Growing Up with SCIENCE®

Third Edition

15

Thermometer–Virus, biological

Marshall Cavendish
Reference
New York

CONTENTS

KEY TO COLOR CODING OF ARTICLES

EARTH, SPACE, AND ENVIRONMENTAL SCIENCES

LIFE SCIENCES AND MEDICINE

MATHEMATICS

PHYSICS AND CHEMISTRY

TECHNOLOGY

PEOPLE

Marshall Cavendish
99 White Plains Road
Tarrytown, NY 10591

www.marshallcavendish.us

Library of Congress Cataloging-in-Publication Data

Growing up with science.— 3rd ed.
    p. cm.
  Includes index.
  Contents: v. 1. Abrasive-Astronomy — v. 2. Atmosphere-Cable television —
v. 3. Cable travel-Cotton — v. 4. Crane-Electricity — v. 5 Electric motor-
Friction — v. 6. Fuel cell-Immune system — v. 7. Induction-Magnetism —
v. 8. Mapmaking-Mining and quarrying — v. 9. Missile and torpedo-Oil
exploration and refining — v. 10. Optics-Plant kingdom — v. 11. Plasma
physics-Radiotherapy — v. 12. Railroad system-Seismology — v. 13.
Semiconductor-Sports — v. 14. Spring-Thermography — v. 15. Thermometer-
Virus, biological — v. 16. Virus, computer-Zoology — v. 17. Index.
  ISBN 0-7614-7505-2 (set)
  ISBN 0-7614-7520-6 (vol. 15)
  1. Science—Encyclopedias.

Q121.G764 2006
503—dc22

                                                    2004049962
                                    09 08 07 06 05 6 5 4 3 2 1

Printed in China

CONSULTANT

Donald R. Franceschetti, Ph.D.

Dunavant Professor at the University of Memphis

Donald R. Franceschetti is a member of the American
Chemical Society, the American Physical Society, the
Cognitive Science Society, the History of Science Society,
and the Society for Neuroscience.

CONTRIBUTORS TO VOLUME 15

Rebecca Clunes   Chris Cooper

Sarah Evans   Tom Jackson

Marshall Cavendish

Editors: Peter Mavrikis and Susan Rescigno

Editorial Director: Paul Bernabeo

Production Manager: Alan Tsai

The Brown Reference Group

Editors: Leon Gray and Simon Hall

Designer: Sarah Williams

Picture Researchers: Susy Forbes and Laila Torsun

Indexer: Kay Ollerenshaw

Illustrators: Darren Awuah and Mark Walker

Managing Editor: Bridget Giles

Art Director: Dave Goodman

Thermometer

Temperature—the property that determines the direction of heat flow between objects—is measured by instruments called thermometers. Various types of thermometers measure the temperature of the air, the human body, and the temperatures produced by chemical reactions.

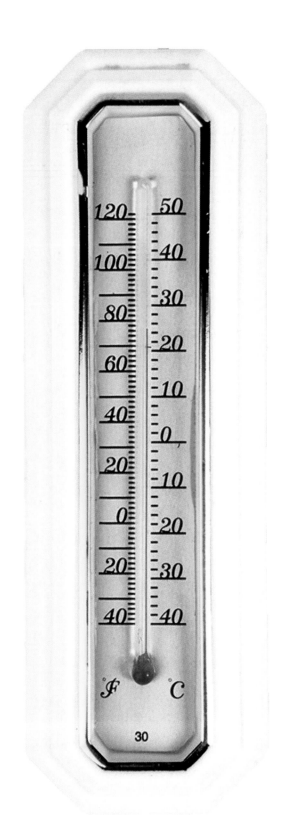

▲ *This bulb thermometer is used to measure the temperature of the atmosphere. It consists of a sealed glass tube containing alcohol (dyed red). Celsius and Fahrenheit temperature scales are marked on either side of the alcohol-filled tube.*

Reading a thermometer to find out the air temperature or taking the temperature of someone who is ill are the most common everyday uses of thermometers. As well as the familiar thermometers used for these tasks, there are many other types of thermometers used in science. Each one has been developed for a particular use.

The history of thermometers

In 1654, Grand Duke Ferdinand II of Tuscany (1610–1670) invented the first accurate thermometer. It was a sealed, liquid-in-glass thermometer, which used alcohol. This was the main type of thermometer used for many years, and liquid-in-glass thermometers are still widely used.

Once thermometers had been invented, one problem was deciding on the best temperature scale to use. It was many years before scientists decided on two main scales. The Fahrenheit temperature scale was devised in 1717 by German physicist Gabriel Fahrenheit (1686–1736), who was working in Amsterdam, Holland. Fahrenheit produced thermometers with mercury as the liquid, and with a scale of 32 degrees as the freezing point of water and 212 degrees as the boiling point of water. By comparison, the Celsius scale uses 0 degrees as the freezing point of water and 100 degrees as the boiling point of water. The Celsius scale is named for its inventor, Swedish astronomer Anders Celsius (1701–1744). It is also called the centigrade scale. Both scales became widely used for thermometers.

Bulb thermometers

The thermometer that is familiar to most people is the clinical bulb thermometer. This is a slender glass tube, containing a liquid, that is placed in the mouth to record body temperature. Bulb thermometers work on the scientific rule that as liquid gets warmer, it expands (pushes outward), and as it gets cooler, it contracts (shrinks).

The liquid in a bulb thermometer is held in a reservoir in the form of a small bulb at the bottom of the glass tube, which gives the thermometer its name. The tube has a scale marked along one side of the liquid-filled tube to read the temperature. When the liquid is heated, for example, because it is placed in the mouth of a person with a fever, it expands and rises up the tube.

The tube is extremely narrow—less than $\frac{1}{20}$ inch (0.5 millimeter) in diameter. Therefore, a small amount of expansion or contraction of the liquid in the bulb, caused by heating or cooling, produces a noticeable rise or fall in its level in the tube.

A limitation of bulb thermometers is that they cannot measure temperatures below the freezing point or above the boiling point of the liquid they contain. Mercury is the most common liquid used in bulb thermometers. For measuring very cold temperatures, mercury is limited by its freezing point of −38°F (−39°C). Alcohol is used for low-temperature applications. Because alcohol is colorless, the liquid is usually dyed red or blue, so it can be seen easily. Alcohol has a lower freezing point than mercury (−170°F or −112°C), but it can measure temperatures only as high as its boiling point of 173°F (78°C).

Maximum-minimum thermometers

Meteorologists (people who study the weather) have to measure the maximum (highest) and minimum (lowest) temperatures during the day, so they use a special thermometer to do this. It has a U-shaped tube with mercury in the middle part and alcohol at each end. One end also has a reservoir for the alcohol.

As the temperature rises, the alcohol expands and pushes the mercury through the tube. The mercury, in turn, pushes a steel marker along a scale. The marker stops at the highest point to which it is pushed, and this shows the maximum temperature during the day.

As the temperature drops, the alcohol contracts. This contraction makes the mercury push a second steel marker on the other side of the tube. When

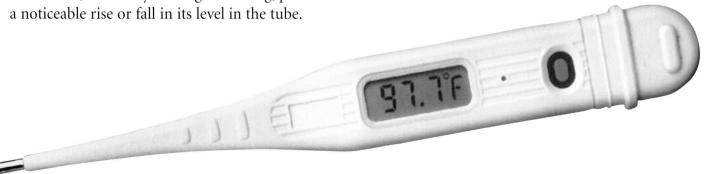

▲ *Digital thermometers are used by health care workers and in the home. They operate electronically using thermistors. Electronic thermometers are much more accurate than bulb thermometers. Their digital displays also make them easier to read.*

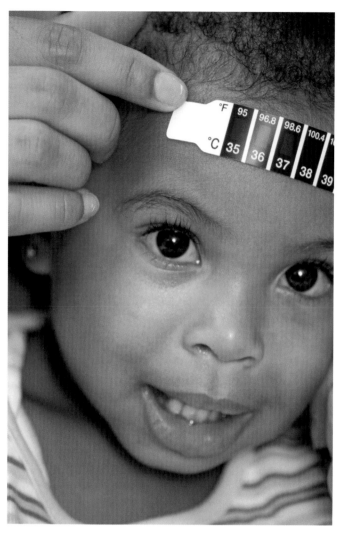

When a constant voltage is applied to these materials, a small current flows that is inversely proportional to the electrical resistance of the material. The value of this current is determined by the temperature of the element. A computer or other circuit converts the current measurement to a temperature, either as a digital display or to make decisions about turning something on or off.

Accurate electrical temperature measurements can also be made with thermocouples. When two wires of dissimilar metals are joined to form a loop, and one junction is kept at a lower temperature than the other, a small voltage difference (measured in microvolts) is created between the junctions. The voltage is a function of the temperature difference.

Noninvasive and highly accurate infrared thermometers, called tympanic thermometers, have also been developed. They can take readings of body temperature by measuring infrared radiation (heat) coming from the ear.

the marker stops, it shows the minimum temperature for the day. The steel markers in the tube must be reset with magnets every day.

Electrical thermometers

Bulb thermometers are often unsuitable for measuring very high or very low temperatures. For these applications, it is now common to measure temperature using electronics. Electrical thermometers are also increasingly used for more regular applications because they have the advantage of being very accurate and easy to read.

The most common electrical sensor is a thermoresistor (or thermistor). It works using the predictable change of electrical resistance in certain metals or semiconductors as their temperature changes. These materials include platinum and oxides of nickel, manganese, or cobalt.

Bimetallic strip thermometers

Another type of simple thermometer is the bimetallic strip thermometer. These consist of two different metals joined at the ends. Brass and invar (iron alloy plus nickel) are often used in this way. Platinum with iridium is another combination.

The paired metals are attached to a pointer. As the temperature changes, each metal expands and contracts at a different rate. So when one expands or contracts faster than the other, the strip bends and moves a pointer along a scale. One use of bimetallic thermometers is to make thermographs, which are charts of temperatures. In this case, the strip is attached to a pen instead of a pointer, and the pen marks the temperatures on a revolving chart.

See also: MERCURY, METAL • TEMPERATURE

Thermostat

Thermostats measure the temperature around them and turn cooling or heating systems on and off. Some thermostats work by using metal strips that bend with heat. Others use the fact that liquids and gases expand and take up more space when they are heated. Refrigerators and central-heating systems use thermostats.

A thermostat is a device that controls the temperature of a heating or cooling system. This automatic control of temperature is needed for refrigerators, central heating and air conditioning systems, cooling systems in automobiles, and in many industrial processes.

One of the earliest examples of a thermostat was designed about 1606 by Dutch inventor Cornelius Drebbel (1572–1633) while working in London. His device controlled an incubator for growing plants from seeds. Hot gases from a furnace heated a water jacket placed around the incubator. The water also heated alcohol in a container, which, when it expanded with heat, pushed down on a column of mercury. The mercury pushed a lever that opened or closed the furnace chimney, so it roughly controlled the temperature.

Bimetallic strips

Instead of using the expansion of liquid, as in early thermostats, modern thermostats make use of the expansion properties of metals. A bimetallic strip is made of two strips of different metals welded together. The metals expand by different amounts when they are heated, and the two sides of the strip become slightly different in length. The strip is forced to bend toward the shorter side, and the amount of bend depends on the temperature.

The bending of the bimetallic strip can be used to directly turn a valve on and off, or it can operate an electric circuit. When the strip touches a metal contact, the electrical current flows. When the strip bends away from the contact, the current stops.

Often, the bimetallic strip in a thermostat is in the form of a coil, which allows the strip a greater range of movement. As the coil is heated, it expands and uncoils, turning a contact attached to its center. As the coil cools, it contracts and recoils, turning the contact in the opposite direction.

The contacts in thermostats are often mercury switches. A mercury switch is a glass vial that contains a small amount of mercury. Mercury is a

▶ *This thermostat is attached to a central-heating system. The thermostat is set to the temperature required. If the house is too cold, the thermostat turns the heating on until the required temperature has been reached.*

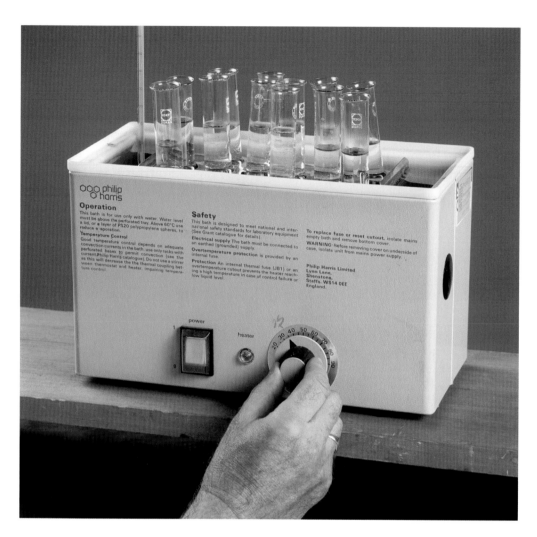

◄ In this water bath full of test tubes, the temperature of the water can be set and maintained using a thermostat dial. This allows scientists to control experiments that need to be carried out at fixed temperatures.

metal that is liquid at normal temperatures. It conducts electricity and flows like water. As the bimetallic coil expands and contracts, it tilts the mercury switch from one side to the other, making and breaking electrical connections.

Inside the glass vial are three wires. One wire runs across the bottom of the vial, so the mercury is always in contact with it. Another wire connects to the left side of the vial. When the vial tilts to the left, the mercury makes contact between this wire and the one on the bottom of the vial. The third wire connects to the right side of the vial. When the vial tilts to the right, the mercury makes contact between this wire and the bottom wire.

Central heating systems usually use a coiled bimetallic strip and mercury switch in the room thermostats that control them. When the temperature dial is twisted to the desired setting, the position of the mercury switch on the bimetallic coil is adjusted. This affects when it will be tilted by the coil and when the heating, or possibly air conditioning, will be turned on.

Other devices

Electrical resistance is another property of a metal that changes with temperature. When the temperature goes up, the resistance increases, and any electrical current flowing decreases. A resistance thermostat is useful for controlling electrical machines as it forms part of the circuit it controls.

All types of thermostats use the principle of feedback. They send information about heat back to the source of heat. Self-regulating devices such as these are known as servomechanisms.

See also: MERCURY, METAL • RESISTANCE • SERVOMECHANISM • TEMPERATURE

Thunderstorm

With bolts of lightning flashing across the sky, sudden claps of thunder, and strong winds and rain, thunderstorms are one of the most spectacular everyday weather disturbances. Most thunderstorms do not last longer than an hour, but a storm at its height makes a big impact.

Scientists believe that as many as 3,500 thunderstorms may be taking place around Earth at any one time. Astronauts in space have described the clouds that circle Earth as being lit up with hundreds of lightning flashes.

Thunder is the immediate result of a bolt of lightning, which comes from electrical charges built up within a type of cloud formation called cumulonimbus clouds. These towering clouds are thick—usually 5 to 7 miles (8 to 12 kilometers) deep—and heavy and dark at their bases. They usually appear on warm, sunny days, when warm air rises from the ground. As it rises, the air cools, and its moisture condenses into water droplets and ice crystals, forming immense, billowing clouds.

Lightning

Although the sound of thunder can be frightening, it is the lightning that is more dangerous. In the United States, one hundred people are killed by lightning every year.

The long zigzag of brilliant white light in the sky is actually a huge charge of electricity. A lightning flash can heat the air in its path to temperatures of 54,000°F (30,000°C)—five times hotter than the surface of the Sun. This heated air spreads out, loses heat, and quickly shrinks. Air rushing in to fill the gap creates the sound of thunder. This can sound like a rumbling noise as thunder sound waves emanate from different parts of a storm.

▼ *This cumulonimbus cloud with a flat top is called a thunderhead. It is caused by strong winds in the stratosphere blowing down on the cloud.*

◄ *Rising air currents separate positive and negative particles in clouds. The air at ground level reacts to the negative cloud layer and becomes positive. Lightning zigzags back and forth until the two opposite charges have canceled each other out.*

Lightning and thunder actually happen together. Because light travels so much faster than sound, however, the lightning is seen first. By counting the seconds between the flash of lightning and the arrival of the sound of thunder, it is possible to judge how far away a thunderstorm is. A gap of 5 seconds is equal to about 1 mile (1.6 kilometers).

How lightning is caused

There is still much that is not known about thunderstorms, but scientists have been able to unlock some of the mysteries surrounding them. Thunderclouds are full of strong electrical charges. When violent currents of air sweep in at the edges of clouds, they separate out negatively and positively charged particles. Ice crystals in the cloud become negatively charged as the air currents cause them to collide, while the air around them is positively charged. Eventually, the top layer of the thundercloud becomes positively charged, while the middle and bottom layers are negatively charged. The ground below the cloud is also positively charged, sometimes even causing people's hair to stand on end.

DID YOU KNOW?

On average, an individual cumulonimbus cloud takes only one hour to take shape, grow, and dissipate. It produces less than 30 minutes of thunder and lightning.

Why lightning strikes

The positive and negative electrical charges are strongly attracted to each other. After a while, the insulating layer of air between the charges cannot keep them apart. In a massive surge of energy, electricity leaps between them in a zigzag pattern. The first sparks usually occur between different parts of the clouds. This is known as cloud-to-cloud lightning. Then lightning occurs between the positive charges on the ground and the negative charges in the cloud, traveling between them at about 270,000 miles (435,000 kilometers) per hour. Sometimes lightning also strikes between clouds and the air. To the human eye, a flash of lightning striking the ground is a single strike. Photographs, however, show that there is usually a "leader" flash to the ground, which is followed by a far more powerful return stroke.

The three most common forms of lightning—forked, branched, and sheet—are in fact three different views of the same flash. Sheet lightning, for example, is simply a lightning flash that is obscured by a cloud. Another form of lightning, ball lightning, is a rare phenomenon that occurs when part of a lightning strike from cloud to ground forms a small, round ball. This ball of light rolls along the ground or bounces in the air, until it either explodes or dissipates.

See *also:* CLOUD • ELECTRICITY • LIGHTNING • RAIN AND RAINFALL • TORNADO

Tidal power

Tidal power is the use of the movement of ocean tides to generate electricity. This renewable source of natural energy is not yet widely used, but new technology could make tidal power an important future source of energy.

As the cost of fossil fuels (coal, oil, and natural gas) rises, power stations that burn these fuels become more expensive to run, making electricity more costly to consumers. A reason for the rising cost of fossil fuels is that the world's supply of them is running out. Many new fossil-fuel reserves are increasingly difficult and costly to exploit.

Another problem with using fossil fuels is pollution. The emissions produced by power stations that burn fossil fuels contribute greatly to atmospheric pollution. So, for many reasons, other ways of generating electricity must be found.

Nuclear energy was once thought to be the long-term answer to the world's power demands. However, the dangerous nature of the radioactive materials used in nuclear power stations still presents serious safety implications. In addition, radioactive waste can also be highly polluting to the environment.

The best energy resources seem to be those presenting few environmental dangers and involving materials that will not run out. Such resources are called renewable energy resources. These include the Sun (solar power), the wind, and the power of moving water (hydroelectric power; HEP).

Power from water

When moving water is used to produce electricity, it is usually done using a system of turbines. A turbine is similar to a propeller.

For hydroelectric power, a large body of water is held behind the wall of a dam and allowed to run as a powerful current over turbines. As the water

▲ This tidal power station on the River Rance in France is one of the oldest and most productive. The tidal range in the estuary is high, and this provides enough flowing water to drive large turbines and generators.

rushes past, the turbines revolve and turn the moving parts of the generators—the rotors. The rotors are powerful magnets, and as they revolve, they induce electrons to move in tightly wound coils of wire around the outside of each generator. These coils make up the stators. An electrical current is made to flow in the stators, which can then be supplied to the local power grid.

Tidal power works on the same principle as a power station built at a dam, but instead of flowing water from a dam, tidal power uses the movement of the ocean tides to turn generators.

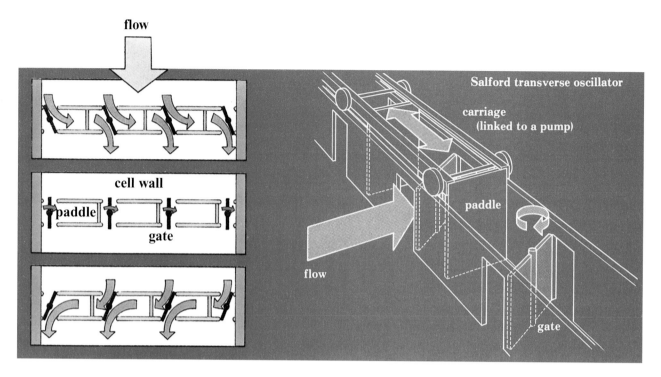

▲ *This diagram shows a Salford transverse oscillator, which is designed to generate tidal power with only a low head of water. Water enters a gate in the barrier and pushes the paddle along until a second gate opens and the first one closes. This directs the water so that it pushes the paddle back again, and so on. The moving paddles operate a pump to push water past a turbine.*

All the oceans of the world are subject to tides. Tides are the movements of bodies of water as they are pulled across Earth's surface by the gravity of the Moon. In smaller seas, such as the Mediterranean, the movement of the tides is hardly noticeable. In large oceans, such as the Atlantic and the Pacific, the water may move many feet up and down the shore with each change of tide.

In the course of a day, there are two high tides and two low tides. These do not occur at the same times each day, as their movement depends on the Moon's cycle.

Building a tidal power station

Solar, wind, and tidal power are free in the sense that it does not cost anything to have that power available, while much money must be spent to drill for oil and gas or to mine for coal. However, neither solar nor tidal power is totally free. The machinery needed to convert these forms of energy into electricity is expensive, and in the case of tidal power, there are many problems in making the system work efficiently. In fact, there are so many problems that there are just a few tidal power stations in the world. The two oldest are at La Rance near St. Malo, in France, and Kislogubsk, in northern Russia. The first and only tidal plant in North America is located in Annapolis Royal by the Bay of Fundy, between New Brunswick and Nova Scotia, in eastern Canada. The Bay of Fundy is home to the world's highest tides.

To build a tidal power station, a barrier must be put across an inlet or river estuary. As the tide rises, water flows into the space behind the barrier, creating a reservoir. As the tide falls, water flows out of the reservoir through a gap in the barrier, driving turbines as it moves.

At the tidal power station at La Rance, the turbines are built to operate whichever way the water is flowing—in or out of the reservoir. As a result, power can be generated for twice as long as if it worked only as the reservoir emptied. This power station also has a system of pumps that help fill the reservoir when the tide does not rise very high. (Tides do not always rise to the same height, and the difference between high and low tide changes throughout the year.)

These pumps operate using off-peak electricity (electricity generated when demand is low), which is cheaper than at times when there is a heavy demand. In this way, cheaper power is used to pump the water into the reservoir for use in generating electricity in periods when demand is high.

The ideal place to build a tidal power station is where there is a wide difference between the levels of high and low tides and where the shape of the coastline is suitable. The difference between the levels of high and low tides is called the tidal range. The tidal range at La Rance, for example, is 44 feet (13.5 meters), which means that as the tide falls, the water level drops an average of 44 feet (13.5 meters). The buildup of water that takes place at high tide is called the head of the water. The best site for generating tidal power is where a wide tidal range results in a large head of water. When the head of water is less than 15 feet (4.6 meters), production of tidal power is less efficient.

The shape of the coastline is important to a tidal power station. The system works best when a barrier can be built across an inlet that will hold a large amount of water behind it. The best type of inlet is one that becomes narrower soon after it leaves the coastline and makes its way inland.

The combination of a good tidal range and the right kind of inlet is not always easy to find, which is one of the reasons that there are few tidal power stations around the world. Two possible sites in North America are at Cook Inlet in Alaska and in the Gulf of California, and there are a few others around the world.

The solution to the problem of the lack of ideal sites is to find methods that will work efficiently at other sites, making wider use of tidal power possible. Scientists have been working on ways, for example, to generate electricity where the head of water is too small to drive a conventional turbine fast enough, or where it is not worth spending large sums of money to build huge dams or barriers.

Flexible barriers

One method, developed in the United States, uses a flexible barrier supported by an inflatable tube stretched across an estuary. As the tide rises, water is forced through a chamber on the seabed. As it passes through this chamber, the water works a piston that pumps air through a flexible pipe running to the land. There, the air drives a turbine that is connected to a generator. This system is useful because the barrier is light and easy to move if ships need to pass into the estuary. Also, because it does not involve much building or engineering work, it is ideal for small-scale operations.

British scientists have taken another approach. They have designed contour rafts, which resemble huge butterflies. These rectangular rafts are connected together by hinges that contain pistons. As waves rock the rafts, they flex the hinges and force the pistons to pump water. The water drives turbines that produce electricity.

◀ *Annapolis Tidal Generating Station in Canada uses its Straflo turbines to generate about 30 million kilowatt-hours per year—enough to power four thousand homes.*

▲ *This tidal-power device uses hydroplanes (water wings). As these are moved up and down by the water stream, they drive hydraulic pumps. The pumps supply high-pressure oil, which is used to drive a generator.*

The Straflo turbine

Another method of tidal-power generation uses specially designed turbines to operate a generator when there is not a large enough head of water to exert the power needed to work an ordinary system.

The Straflo turbine has been designed for this purpose. It makes use of the fact that the outer tips of a turbine's blades revolve faster than the parts nearest the center. In the same position, and with the same amount and speed of water turning the turbines, the tips of longer blades will revolve faster than those of shorter ones. The Straflo turbine has longer blades, with the generator rotor carried on a ring mounted on the ends of the turbine blades. So, in places where a normal turbine would not turn fast enough—and the generator rotor, therefore, would not revolve fast enough—the Straflo system might be able to generate electricity.

Gates and paddles

Another promising method being developed involves the use of gates and paddles in a barrier across an estuary or inlet. As the water moves, it passes through gates in the barrier. Each gate is set at right angles to the direction in which the water flows. As the water enters the gate, it pushes a paddle to one side and rotates the gate slightly. The water is forced to the other side of the paddle and flows back the way it came. This moves the gate back to its original position, and the whole process can start again. The motion of the paddle is linked to a pump that drives water through a turbine to generate electricity in the usual way. This system does not need a large head of water, and it works both as the tide comes in and as it goes out. Any number of gates and paddles can be used, depending on the size of the power station required.

Looking to the future

It is obvious that there is a great need for more sources of clean, renewable energy, and that tidal power holds potential. Development of tidal-power systems with potential for widespread use has been slow; and their performance, often disappointing. Given further development, however, it is hoped that many more areas around the world can take advantage of this inexhaustible provider of power.

See also: DAM • MOON • POWER GENERATION AND DISTRIBUTION • SOLAR ENERGY • TIDE • TURBINE • WINDMILL AND WIND PUMP

Tide

Tides are twice-daily rises and falls in the levels of the seas. They occur throughout the oceans but are seen most easily on coasts. Lakes and ponds also experience miniature tides. The regular variation in water levels has a great effect not only on shipping and navigation, but also on wildlife—animals feed and rest according to the tides.

The waters of the oceans are constantly on the move. As Earth turns within the gravitational fields of the Sun and Moon, a pull is exerted on the oceans' waters. This force has little effect on solid objects on Earth. Ocean water is fluid, however, and it moves toward the points of the strongest and weakest gravitational pull. As a result, the ocean waters bulge outward at two points, and it is these bulges that cause the high water levels, which are known as high tides.

One bulge is directly beneath the Moon, while the other is on the opposite side of the globe. By contrast, there are two other points at right angles to the bulges where the waters are flattened. At these points there are low tides.

The bulges can be thought of as waves that sweep around Earth in the same direction that Earth spins on its axis. The Moon orbits Earth in the same direction as Earth spins on its axis. It takes 24 hours and 50 minutes for the Moon to be overhead at the same place. There are roughly two high tides and two low tides per day at any given place, but they occur at times that change from day to day. So the interval between two successive high tides is not 12 hours, but 12 hours and 25 minutes. As a result, most countries publish tide tables showing the times of high and low tides at the main ports for a year in advance.

▼ *The seas are in constant motion. Winds generate waves and ripples, while the tides cause a regular rise and fall of the water. Tides are seen most prominently along coasts and in harbors and bays.*

In the open sea, the tidal range (the difference between high and low tide) is only 1 to 2 feet (0.3–0.6 meter). In narrow tidal estuaries, however, it may be 40 to 50 feet (12 to 15 meters). So-called tidal waves, which are more correctly called tsunamis, have nothing to do with tides. They are caused by earthquakes or other Earth movements.

High and low tides

The Sun is much farther away from Earth than the Moon. However, the Sun's far greater mass also causes tides, although these are a little less than half of the height of tides caused by the Moon. Every 28 days, the Sun, Moon, and Earth are in line, and the gravitational forces of the Sun and the Moon are combined. This is the time of the spring tides, when the tidal range is greatest. Spring tides occur during the full moon and new moon. When the Sun,

▼ *The beach at Lyme Regis, England, is exposed at low tide. The water marks on the breakwaters below the houses indicate how high the water rises at high tide.*

DID YOU KNOW?

The tides were first explained by English physicist Isaac Newton (1642–1727). He developed a theory of gravity, stating that the Moon's gravity attracts Earth, creating a bulge in Earth's sea surface just below the Moon.

Earth, and Moon form a right angle, however, the gravitational forces of the Sun and Moon oppose each other. This is the time of the neap tides, when the tidal range is lowest. Neap tides occur when the Moon is in its first and third quarters.

The idea that tides are waves that move around the world is not an accurate description. In reality, each ocean basin or sea acts like a separate container of water, with its own natural period of oscillation. This is the time it takes for a disturbance in the water to travel from one end to the other. For example, bath water can be made to oscillate back and forth with a

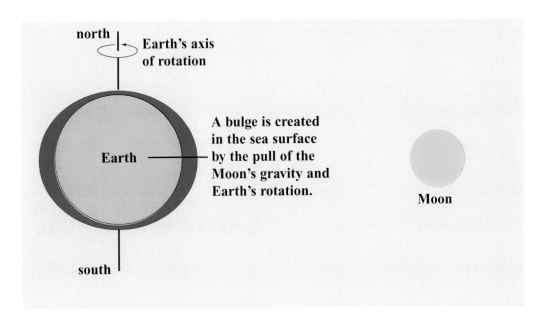

north — Earth's axis of rotation

Earth

A bulge is created in the sea surface by the pull of the Moon's gravity and Earth's rotation.

Moon

south

◄ *These illustrations show the influence of the Moon, Sun, and Earth's rotation on Earth's tides. The top illustration shows the tidal pull caused by the Moon's gravity. The bottom illustration shows how the neap and spring tides occur.*

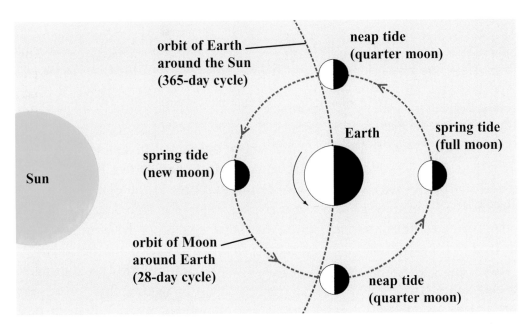

orbit of Earth around the Sun (365-day cycle)

neap tide (quarter moon)

Earth

spring tide (new moon)

spring tide (full moon)

Sun

orbit of Moon around Earth (28-day cycle)

neap tide (quarter moon)

characteristic frequency when it is disturbed. The size of the oscillation can be increased with an added push or decreased by working against it.

In the same way, the water in particular oceans or seas reacts differently to the frequency of the gravitational tidal pull. This depends on whether the gravitational tidal pull coincides with the natural frequency of oscillation (called the harmonics) of the region or basin. The natural period of oscillation of Lake Erie in North America, for example, is 14 hours. This is not very different from the period of 12 hours 25 minutes in the oceans. Lake Erie has a tidal range of 3⁄10 inches (8 centimeters). However, Lake Baikal in Russia has a period of 4½ hours and a tidal range of only ⅗ inch (1.5 centimeters). Some almost enclosed seas, such as the Baltic and the Mediterranean seas, are nearly tideless because of their harmonics.

Other seas that are connected to oceans by broad stretches of water, such as the North Sea, have much larger tidal ranges. The greatest tidal range occurs in the funnel-shaped Bay of Fundy, which separates the peninsula of Nova Scotia from the mainland Canadian province of New Brunswick. There, the average spring tide range is 45½ feet (14.5 meters), with an extreme range of 53½ feet (16.3 meters).

▲ *Morecambe Bay in northeastern England is a wide bay with a large area of mud flats between the high and low tide marks. The bay is notoriously dangerous, with quicksand and very fast rising tides.*

Tides that are channeled into narrow estuaries can push saltwater upstream over the fresh river water, forming a wall of water. These features are called bores. They occur in many rivers, but the largest bore occurs on the Tsien-Tang Kiang River estuary in China. On occasion, it can reach 26 feet (8 meters) high in an estuary that is several miles wide. Like ocean currents and the winds, tides veer to the right in the Northern Hemisphere and to the left in the Southern Hemisphere due to Earth's rotation. When a tide flows into a nearly enclosed sea, this Coriolis force can make the tides circle around a point in the sea where the surface is at a constant height.

Regions with strong tidal currents are generally scoured and cleansed of industrial and domestic wastes. Tidal currents take wastes away from polluted harbors and carry them out to sea. The coastal waters of seas that are almost without tides, such as those in the Mediterranean Sea, tend to be severely polluted.

Tidal power

In France, the tides have been used to generate electricity. Across the Rance River estuary, where the tidal range is more than 40 feet (12 meters), a dam has been built. Gates in the dam open when the tide is rising and close at high water. The water is then stored above the dam to drive turbines.

The same principle was used for hundreds of years in tide mills, where the tide was allowed to flood a reservoir. At these mills, floodgates were then closed just after high water. When the tide went down, the water was released from the reservoir to drive the mill wheels. By using a head of water, more power was produced than if the tide had flowed out at the normal rate.

Generating electricity from the tides began in 1966, but tidal energy will only make a small contribution to the world's energy crisis. This is largely because the head of water is about ten times less than that of a normal hydroelectric station. As a result, large and costly turbines must be used.

See also: DAM • ENERGY • MOON • TIDAL POWER • TSUNAMI

Timber industry

Wood is one of the most important materials on Earth. It is useful not only as lumber for home building and furniture making, but also to make paper, cardboard, and many other materials. The business of growing trees and harvesting them for their wood is known as the timber industry.

People have used timber from the forests for building and for fuel from the earliest times. In some parts of the world, wood and the charcoal made from wood is burned in large amounts every day for cooking, heating water, and keeping people warm. In the developed world, the largest single use for wood is in construction work—especially the building of homes. Other major users of wood are manufacturers of furniture, crates and boxes, paper, and plywood.

With such a demand for trees, it is important to make sure the world's supply of lumber does not run out. Trees take many years to grow large enough to supply lumber. If they are used up faster than they can be replaced, the world may run short of lumber. Also, Earth's climate would be seriously affected by the absence of forests.

There are two types of timber. Softwoods are used in building and papermaking and in most other areas where large amounts of wood are needed. Hardwoods are used mainly for furniture.

Softwoods

Softwoods are from coniferous (evergreen) trees—usually pine, cedar, fir, cypress, and spruce. They grow in great numbers in many parts of the world, but particularly in Russia, Finland, Sweden, the United States, and Canada.

Trees for use by the timber industry are grown commercially, as a crop. When trees are felled, new trees are planted in their places. These trees start their lives as seedlings in the forest nursery and are transplanted into the forest. There they are still tended, thinned out as they grow larger and need more space, and sprayed to protect them from pests and disease. Smaller trees removed in the thinning process can be used, for example, as fencing stakes.

▶ *The vast forests of Vancouver Island in Canada support a huge timber industry. The trees are coniferous (evergreen) trees. These softwood trees grow more quickly than hardwood trees, so the forests are easier to sustain with replanting. An area of replanted forest could be ready for felling within fifty years.*

One of the greatest dangers to forests is fire. In hot, dry weather, a forest fire can easily be started by accident, and many square miles of trees will be destroyed. In managed forests, watchtowers are built on high ground to spot fires. At especially dry periods of the year, these towers are staffed by people whose job it is to watch carefully for fires. When a fire does break out, firefighting aircraft may be used to help firefighters on the ground.

Hardwoods

Hardwoods come from deciduous (leaf-shedding) trees such as ash, oak, beech, cottonwood, gum, maple, walnut, willow, and yellow poplar, and from Asian, African, and South American tropical trees. Among the best-known tropical hardwoods are ebony, mahogany, and teak. As these have become scarcer over the years, other, less-familiar varieties are used as well.

Hardwoods are used mainly for making furniture and floors and are valued for their appearance. It is the color and the pattern of the grain of these woods that are particularly desired. Hardwoods are taken from natural forests rather than being grown in plantations like softwoods. Such forests must be managed carefully because many hardwood trees can take several centuries to grow to maturity.

Logging

In the past, trees were cut down using axes, which was slow, hard work. Now most felling, as it is called, is done with chain saws, even in poorer countries. Chain saws are power saws with cutting teeth on a chain. First, a notch is cut on the side of the trunk facing the direction of the fall. The rest of the cutting is then done from the other side. Lumberjacks are able to fell trees accurately without risking damage to other trees or equipment.

After the tree has been felled, the top and all the branches are taken off, and the tree is cut up into logs. The logs are hauled to trucks equipped with lifting gear. Hauling may be done using tractors or horses. In some of Asia's teak forests, elephants are used. In Canadian forests, aerial cableways carry logs to collection points.

The logs are then taken to sawmills. The logs may be carried by road or rail, but in many parts of the world, they are transported by river. The logs are simply floated downstream to the sawmills or are tied together as rafts and towed there. In northern countries, the rivers freeze over in winter. The logs are stacked on the ice, and when it melts, they are carried along by the current. Water is the most convenient and economic method of transporting large numbers of heavy logs.

◄ *A large vehicle-mounted chain saw is being used to fell trees in Scotland. Mechanization allows trees to be felled more quickly, easily, and safely than by using hand-operated saws.*

◀ This huge sawmill is in Alaska. Felled trees are floated down rivers to a large holding basin. When they are required, cranes lift the logs from the water, and they are sent through the plant for processing into lumber.

At the sawmill

In countries where there is a large timber industry, sawmills are highly mechanized and deal with thousands of logs every day. Logs that have been floated down to the sawmill are stored in large ponds. The bark is then removed by bark-stripping machines, and the logs are sorted for size and quality before being brought into the mill.

In a modern sawmill, conveyors move logs from one operation to the next. The whole process is highly automated. An operator, called a sawyer, sits at a control panel and decides the best way to cut each log. Pushbutton controls send the log to the saw that will cut it in the way that will produce the best planks.

Logs are cut with mechanized saws, of which there are several kinds. The frame saw has several parallel saws on a frame. They all make cuts in the log at the same time for fast and accurate production of boards.

A band saw is used in some mills. A band saw has a long saw belt that travels around two large pulley wheels at high speed. Circular saws are used in smaller sawmills and also when logs have to be cut crosswise instead of lengthwise into planks.

The thickness of a saw and its tooth-set (how the teeth are positioned) determine the amount of wood that will be wasted in the form of sawdust and also the length of time that a saw will last. The right saw must be chosen for each type of wood, and the saw itself must be frequently maintained by a "saw doctor."

Once the logs have been cut into boards, the wood is carried to edging machines, which cut the boards to the right width. In many mills, the waste wood goes automatically to burners that help power the sawmill.

The cut boards are then carried by conveyor to people called brackers, whose job it is to check each piece for faults, such as knots or twists or other defects created by the way in which the wood has grown. They also look for cupping, which is the name given to the way some boards will curve widthwise. Faults can affect the value of the wood, so each piece must be clearly marked with its grade.

The wood must also be graded for strength. An expert grader can do this just by looking at it, but there are machines that, with the help of computers, can test wood for strength, and these are usually used. In some countries, laws require machine testing.

Finally, the pieces of wood are sorted into different sizes and stacked up to be dried. The wood must be dried until the moisture content makes up no more than 24 percent of its weight. This drying can be done simply by allowing air to circulate around the wood, but it can be done much faster using heated kilns.

◄ *This forestry worker is planting new saplings in Vancouver, Canada. Careful forest management and replanting is essential to maintaining the world's forests.*

Deforestation is most common in the developing countries. To make money, these countries often rely on producing cash crops for export. They can earn the most money from their land by growing crops such as tobacco or cotton, or by cattle ranching. They therefore take land from farmers for these uses, forcing the farmers to go elsewhere and cut down more forests to grow food. Developing countries can also sell lumber for cash, and it is tempting for them to cut too much.

When forests disappear, local people suffer. Many people no longer have enough wood for heating or cooking. When wood is too scarce to use for boiling water, disease takes hold and people die.

Deforestation affects all of humankind. Tropical forests contain approximately five billion species of plants and animals, many of which are being made extinct before they are even discovered. Less than one percent of tropical forest plants have been tested for potential medicines, yet that small number has produced drugs to treat diseases such as glaucoma, heart disease, and cancer. Deforestation also increases the amount of carbon dioxide in the air, contributing to global warming.

Lumber yards

Once the wood is dry, it is taken to lumber yards, where it can be sold to builders and other users. The wood may have to be planed, cut, or molded to suit the job for which it is required. If wood is to be used indoors, it will have to be dried out further in kilns until the moisture content is as low as 12 percent. Wood shrinks as it dries. It is therefore important to ensure that wood that for use inside buildings is already dry enough, so no further shrinkage will occur in the warm atmosphere of a home or office. Insufficient drying is the reason that some wood warps after it has been used.

Forestry

Forestry scientists study how trees and forests grow. They try to protect forests from fires, plant diseases, and, most of all, from people. Cutting down trees in one place can affect people all over the world. Trees keep the amount of carbon dioxide in the atmosphere in check and thus play an important part in regulating Earth's climate.

The biggest problem forestry scientists face in the twenty-first century is the destruction of tropical forests. Photos of Earth from the Landsat satellite show that about 9 million acres (4 million hectares) of forest are disappearing each year. The destruction of forests is called deforestation.

Helping the forests regrow

Another problem with deforestation is that deforested land can lose its fertility and become useless if it is not carefully managed. Nutrients once generated by decaying forest vegetation no longer enter the soil. Researchers are trying to find ways to grow new forests in areas of old, cleared forest. Forestry scientists in Costa Rica, for example, have tested more than 150 species of trees to see which are best suited to reforest former cattle pastures. Other scientists have helped developing countries create sustainable policies that encourage villagers to plant new forests.

See also: GLOBAL WARMING • PAPER AND PAPERMAKING • WOODWORKING

Time

Everyone is aware that time passes, but even so, it is impossible to say exactly what time is. Over the centuries, scientists have discovered ways to measure time, enabling people to structure their everyday lives. However, time is still the subject of major scientific investigations.

People have always experienced time passing in a regular, ordered way. Since ancient times, people have observed the natural cycles, such as life and death, day and night, and winter and summer. However, time remains mysterious because it is such a difficult concept to define. Some ancient Greek philosophers believed that time was an illusion, and reality was motionless. Many scientists have also believed that time is absolute and unchanging. In modern times, people closely monitor time as they live their daily lives.

The early measurements of time developed out of watching the movements of the Sun, Moon, and stars. As people realized that these movements were repeated, they used them, for example, to assess the right time to plant crops. The ancient Egyptians predicted the annual flooding of the Nile, which always took place a few days after the rising of Sirius, the brightest star in the sky.

From their observations, Egyptian astronomers produced a calendar based on the 365-day year. By studying Sirius, they noticed that the year was actually 365¼ days long. This is called a solar year; it is the time it takes Earth to orbit the Sun.

The Romans, who had used a lunar calendar (based on the time between full moons), adopted this solar calendar in 45 BCE. It was called the Julian calendar because it was introduced by Roman statesman Julius Caesar (100–44 BCE). To try to avoid the problem of the extra day, three years would run for 365 days, and every fourth year would have an extra day. However, the solar year is 365.242199 days long, not 365.25, and so the Roman calendar was actually 11 minutes too long. This may not seem like much, but over hundreds of years, the calendar was in error by several days.

In 1582, Pope Gregory XIII (1502–1585) corrected the situation. By then the calendar was 10 days off, so he decreed that October 5, 1582, would become October 15. He also said that century years would be leap years only if they were divisible by four hundred. This keeps the Gregorian calendar accurate to 26 seconds a year. It is the Gregorian calendar that is still used universally.

▶ *The hourglass is one of the oldest devices for measuring time. Medieval sailors used it to mark the passing of each hour to help them navigate the seas.*

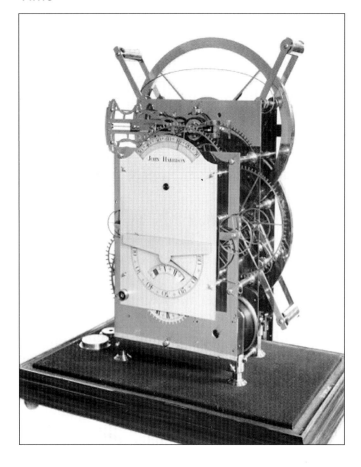

onto a scale marked in hours. As the Sun moves across the sky during the day, the shadow moves around the scale.

Another early way to measure time was with the hourglass (still used by some cooks). It takes exactly one hour for sand in a glass bulb to trickle through a narrow passage into a matching glass bulb below. The clepsydra, called a water clock, was an ancient device that measured time by the regulated flow of water through a small opening.

Mechanical clocks driven by weights were eventually developed. The falling weight was attached to a rope wound around a drum, and as the weight fell, it turned the drum. The revolving drum then worked a system of gears, which moved the hands of the clock. Spring-driven clocks appeared in the late fifteenth century, but the pendulum clock was not invented until the middle of the seventeenth century. Quality pendulum clocks are now accurate to one-thousandth of a second a day.

During the sixteenth and seventeenth centuries, accurate timepieces, called chronometers, were invented. These were needed by sailors to navigate their vessels accurately.

Sidereal and solar time

The Egyptians noticed that the time it takes for Earth to revolve around its axis is always the same if measured against the stars but varies if measured against the Sun. Time based on observations of stars is called sidereal time, and time measured against the Sun is called solar time.

The length of a solar day varies because of the tilt of Earth's axis, the elliptical (oval) shape of its orbit, and its changing speed across its orbit. So the mean (average) solar day is used to make up for this irregularity. Mean solar time can vary from actual solar time by as much as 16 minutes.

A sidereal day is 3 minutes and 56 seconds shorter than a mean solar day. This difference between the solar time and mean time is called the "equation of time." Here the word *equation* means "that which is needed to make things equal."

Early clocks

One of the earliest devices for measuring time was the sundial, known to the ancient Egyptians. A simple sundial has a shaft that casts a shadow

---

DID YOU KNOW?

In 1583, Italian astronomer, mathematician, and physicist Galileo Galilei (1564–1642) made an observation that led to the increased accuracy of mechanical clocks. He watched a chandelier swinging in a cathedral in Pisa, Italy, and timed it by feeling his pulse. He noticed that however far it swung, it took the same time to move back and forth. Galileo experimented with a pendulum and found that the time of swing was directly related to the length of the pendulum. He had discovered one of the first reliable means of timekeeping.

Modern clocks

Clocks and watches with mechanical drives are still made. They could be waterproof, shockproof, antimagnetic, self-winding, or run by electricity. In terms of accuracy, however, mechanical clocks and watches are far behind the electronic timepieces produced by modern technology.

Quartz crystals were first used to drive clocks in 1929, and they are now used in wristwatches as well. Quartz crystals exhibit a property called piezo-electricity. When compressed in a certain way, the crystals generate electrical current. The first quartz clocks were ten times more accurate than the best pendulum clocks, and now they are even better.

Atomic clocks are even more accurate than quartz. Atomic clocks are precision timekeeping devices used in laboratories and in space-satellite communications. They are driven by the atomic vibrations of the metallic element cesium, and they are accurate to within one-millionth of a second per day. In fact, the standard unit of time, the second, is now based on the average time of several cesium atomic clocks around the world. Scientists are working on using other kinds of atoms for atomic clocks. Such clocks—based on hydrogen or beryllium atoms—could be thousands of times more accurate even than today's cesium clocks.

Time zones

The constant turning of Earth on its axis means that sunrises and sunsets do not happen at exactly the same time all over the world. One area's morning is another area's afternoon, midday in one country is midnight in another, and so on. So clocks in different parts of the world show their own local times rather than the same time.

To avoid the confusion that would result if every town had its own sun time, worldwide time zones were set. All locations in a zone keep the same time, and there is a difference of an hour between that zone and the next. The zone to the east is one hour ahead in time, and the zone to the west is one hour behind. Continental United States, for example, is divided into four time zones—Eastern, Central,

▼ *This is the first atomic clock. When it was developed in 1955, it was the most accurate timekeeper in the world. Atomic clocks measure time as natural vibrations of cesium atoms.*

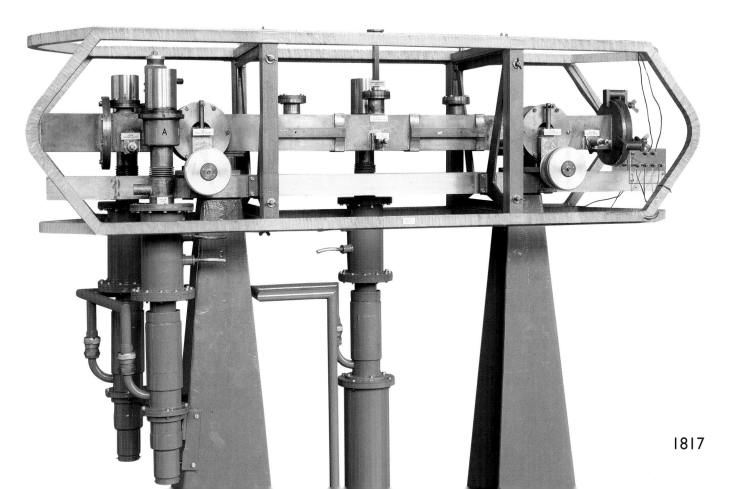

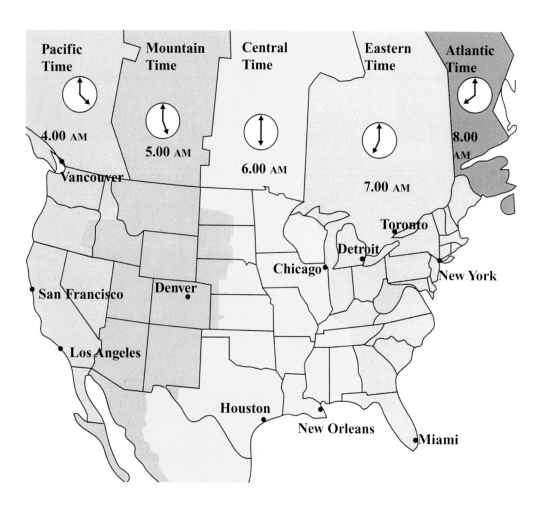

Pacific Time
4.00 AM
Vancouver

Mountain Time
5.00 AM

Central Time
6.00 AM

Eastern Time
7.00 AM

Atlantic Time
8.00 AM

San Francisco

Denver

Chicago

Detroit

Toronto

New York

Los Angeles

Houston

New Orleans

Miami

◄ *This map shows the time zones of mainland United States and part of Canada. In principle, each time zone should have a width of 15 degrees longitude. To avoid dividing communities, however, the zone borders tend to follow state boundaries.*

Mountain, and Pacific. With an hour's difference between each zone, it is easy to figure out that when it is 7 AM in New York, it is 6 AM in Houston, 5 AM in Denver, and 4 AM in Los Angeles.

Time zones were established in 1884. By international agreement, Greenwich, England, was chosen as the place of mean, or meridian, time because it is situated at the meridian line (zero degrees longitude). For every 15 degrees of longitude traveled east or west from the meridian line, time is advanced or set back by one hour.

Modern theories of time

Accurate measurement of time has become increasingly important, particularly for scientific purposes. Despite major advances, however, many questions about time remain unresolved. The work of German-born U.S. physicist Albert Einstein (1879–1955) overturned many of the historical theories about time. Einstein challenged the idea that time is absolute, ideal, and unchanging. He

observed that the speed of light is the same for all observers (186,000 miles or 300,000 kilometers per second). As a consequence, time is not constant—clocks run at different rates for different observers, depending on the relative motion of the clocks and the observers. For example, to an observer on the surface of Earth, the clock in a spaceship passing by at high speed runs slower than a clock on Earth. This slowing of time is called time dilation.

The theory of relativity predicted that clocks run slower in the presence of a gravitational field. For example, a clock in space runs faster than an identical clock on Earth. Modern physics treats time as a feature of space-time, a notion that challenges commonsense perceptions of time as being constant and flowing in one direction—forward. Some scientists suggest that time may actually run backward under certain conditions.

See also: EARTH • ORBIT • TIMEKEEPING DEVICE

Timekeeping device

Finding ways to tell the time has been challenging people for thousands of years. Only in the last few centuries have timekeeping devices been created that could tell the time with any great accuracy. Atomic clocks can now measure time to within one second in over one billion years.

Early people used natural divisions of time, such as the year, the seasons, and the day. The length of these time divisions depended on the movements of the Sun, Moon, and Earth. When the day came to be divided into smaller units, with hours and minutes, the use of more accurate timekeeping clocks and watches was needed.

The earliest clocks

The ancient Egyptians invented the shadow clock, or sundial, to tell the time. The early sundial consisted of a rod placed upright in the ground. As the Sun moved across the sky, it caused the shadow of the rod to change length and position throughout the day. The moving shadow passed over a scale marked on the ground, which enabled the time of day to be seen. A problem with sundials, however, was that they were of no use at night or on days when clouds covered the Sun.

The Egyptians invented the clepsydra (also called the water clock) in 1500 BCE. The clepsydra worked by an arrangement of water containers. In one common design, a large upper container kept a smaller container constantly full with water. Because the smaller container was always full, the pressure of the water inside it remained the same. Water would, therefore, drip out of a spout from the container at a constant rate. The dripping water filled a final, lower vessel containing a floating pointer. As the vessel filled with water, the pointer would rise up a calibrated time scale. Once the

▲ *Traditional mechanical clocks, such as the one in this picture, are inaccurate devices. Most modern clocks work using electrically powered quartz mechanisms.*

lower vessel was full, it was emptied and the clock was reset. Various versions of these water clocks were used throughout the Middle East, China, and Europe until as late as 1400 CE.

After the clepsydra came the sand timer, or hourglass. Invented in Europe about 1200 CE, the sand timer used the flow of sand through a narrow-waisted glass container to indicate the passing of a fixed period of time—often an hour, hence the name. Other versions contained water or mercury.

MECHANICAL CLOCKS AND WATCHES

By the Middle Ages, people wanted to make more accurate timekeeping devices. The first mechanical clock appeared in Europe around 1275. Instead of showing the time on a dial, it struck a single note on a bell every hour (the term *clock* evolved from the Latin *clocca*, meaning "bell"), which worked by a falling weight pulling a wheel around.

Soon after the invention of the mechanical clock, this mechanism was divided into three separate parts: the escapement, the striking train, and the alarm. The escapement controlled the speed at which the clock ran, the striking train sounded the hours on a bell, and the alarm mechanism rang a bell at a chosen time. The escapement comprised a bar that rocked back and forth to interrupt the turning of a toothed balance wheel. A pair of weights controlled the rocking of the bar and, hence, the running of the clock. The toothed wheel was connected to a hand or dial to show the time.

Improvements

The first major improvement to striking clocks was to make them strike the correct number of times for each hour. An early system was invented in Italy about 1330. A better system was invented in 1676 by English priest and clockmaker Reverend Edward Barlow (1636–1716). His system made repeating clocks possible. Repeating clocks repeat the last hour struck when a cord at the side of the clock is

pulled. This was useful for finding the approximate time in the dark. More advanced clocks repeated the last quarter-hour and, sometimes, even chimed the last minute to give a more accurate indication of the time.

Spring drive

Until about 1475, all clocks worked by the use of weights and, therefore, they could not be carried around. If moved, clocks had to be carefully set up again. Then someone thought of using a coiled spring to drive the mechanism. Coiled springs had been used in door locks since 1440. Springs made it possible to reduce the size of clocks, resulting in the development of portable clocks and, eventually, the first watches. However, a problem with early spring-driven clocks was that the balance wheel tended to change speed as the spring expanded or contracted with changing temperature.

Precision timekeeping

A great advance in clock accuracy came in the 1650s when Dutch scientist Christiaan Huygens (1629–1695) invented the first practical pendulum clock. The regular swinging of the pendulum controlled the escapement and thus regulated the clock. In the 1670s, English clockmaker William Clement designed an escapement (called the anchor, or recoil, escapement) for use with the pendulum clock. It allowed a much longer and more accurate pendulum to be used. As a result, Clement was able to reduce the error of a clock from about 15 minutes to 20 seconds per day. With such accuracy available, the use of minute and second hands soon became widespread. For several centuries before, many clocks had only one hand indicating the hours or quarter-hours on the dial.

Chronometer

The invention of the magnetic compass helped seafarers to fix their latitude (east–west position) at sea. As late as the eighteenth century, however,

◀ *English clockmaker John Harrison (1693–1776) was the pioneer of the first accurate, portable clocks, which he called chronometers.*

▲ *Electrical timekeeping devices can include an array of different functions, such as alarms, calendars, and stopwatches, yet be small enough to wear on the wrist.*

there was no workable way to find the longitude (east-west position). The chief problem was that clocks were simply not good enough for use at sea. A ship's motion made pendulums work irregularly, and the extremes of temperature encountered made them expand and contract by large amounts, making them less accurate. Yet the exact time had to be known in order to calculate longitude.

In 1714, there was a terrible shipwreck off the southwestern coast of England. The British government decided to offer a cash reward to anyone who invented an instrument to find longitude.

After several attempts, English clockmaker John Harrison (1693–1776) succeeded in inventing such an instrument. He made his first device, which he called a chronometer, in 1735, and it became known as the H_1. Harrison based it on the gridiron pendulum, which he had invented earlier. This pendulum was made of brass and steel to take advantage of the fact that each metal expands at a different rate as the temperature changes. The

expansion rate of brass compensated for the different expansion rate of steel, keeping the pendulum the same length and, therefore, swinging exactly in time.

To overcome the problems of motion, the H_1 had two large balances. The balance arms acted against springs, so any outside motion of the ship was canceled out by the inside motion of the instrument. The H_1 worked during a short trial, but the government was not convinced of its reliability for longer journeys, so Harrison started building his next device. The H_2 was better, but the government still did not think it was worth the reward, so Harrison went to work on the H_3.

The H_3 was made with a spring instead of a pendulum. To overcome the problem of temperature change in springs, Harrison fitted the spring with a temperature-compensating bimetallic adjuster. As the temperature changed, the expansion and contraction of the bimetallic adjuster altered the length of the spring, keeping the chronometer accurate. Harrison used the bimetallic adjuster again in his final chronometer, the H_4. This instrument was both better and smaller, measuring only 5 inches (13 centimeters) in diameter.

The H_4 proved successful on a long voyage to the West Indies, losing less than 15 seconds in the five months of the journey. At last, mariners had an accurate instrument to find their longitudinal position at sea. In 1773, when Harrison was 80 years old, he finally received the reward.

Mechanical watches

Mechanical watches are driven by a coiled mainspring. A balance wheel spins back and forth to regulate the speed at which an escape wheel moves around in steps to control the speed of the watch.

The first truly portable watches were made in the early sixteenth century. Pieces of hog's bristle were used to give the balance wheel the spring it required. These early watches were poor timekeepers and had only one hand, which showed the hours. More accurate watches appeared in the late seventeenth century, and it was then that a minute hand was added. One great improvement made during this period was the introduction of the hairspring. This fine, coiled spring helped make the balance wheel move back and forth with greater regularity. Then, in 1759, English watchmaker Thomas Mudge (1715–1794) invented a more accurate type of escapement called the lever. The lever escapements found in modern high-grade watches are based on Mudge's design.

However, John Harisson's pocket-size H_4, also completed in 1759, was more accurate still, and set the standard for mechanical watches to follow.

Since the early eighteenth century, jeweled bearings made from ruby have been used in watches. This hard material can support the main moving parts without being worn by the constant rubbing, so the watch lasts longer. Even better reliability can be obtained from an electronic watches and clocks, however, which may have no moving parts at all.

MODERN CLOCKS AND WATCHES

During the twentieth century, inventors steadily improved the accuracy of clocks and watches. In 1921, British engineer William Shortt (1881–1971) developed a clock that was accurate to within one-tenth of a second per year. Shortt's clock was partly electric and had two pendulums—one regulating the other. Some modern clocks, however, are hundreds of times more accurate.

In recent years, electric and electronic clocks have become extremely popular. The first watches driven by electrical power instead of a coiled spring appeared in the 1950s. Pulses of electricity induced a magnetic field to push a balance wheel to keep it moving. The source of power was a tiny electric cell. In some watches of the 1960s, the balance-wheel system was replaced by a tiny tuning fork. This, too, was kept vibrating by means of a magnetic field. In both types of watch, mechanical hands moved over a dial, as in a mechanical watch.

Most modern electric clocks contain a quartz crystal (a form of silicon dioxide; SiO_2). It was discovered that when an electrical current is sent through quartz, it vibrates at an almost constant frequency (number of vibrations per second). This

▲ *Handheld stopwatches such as this one are used for measuring the time of sports races and other events. Many modern stopwatches are digital and contain small computers that can record and compare times.*

is called the piezoelectric effect and can be used to regulate a clock. Artificial quartz is used because it can be made with exactly the frequency required, usually 32,768 hertz (32,768 vibrations per second).

Some types of quartz clocks and watches contain a small motor that drives hour and minute hands around. In others, the time is displayed in a digital format (as numbers). Some digital watches display time in both forms. The day and date are also usually displayed, and the instrument may act as a stopwatch and alarm.

Atomic clocks

In 1945, U.S. physicist Isidor Rabi (1898–1988), suggested that a clock could be regulated using a technique called atomic beam magnetic resonance, which he had developed in the 1930s. Using Rabi's technique, the U.S. National Bureau of Standards developed the world's first atomic clock in 1949.

An atomic clock operates by exposing atoms to microwaves until they vibrate at one of their resonant frequencies and then by counting the corresponding cycles as a measure of time. The first atomic clock used the ammonia molecule (NH_3) as the source of vibrations, but later devices used cesium atoms. Cesium-atom clocks measure resonant frequencies with an accuracy of 2 to 3 parts in 10^{14} hertz. This corresponds to a time measurement accuracy of 2 nanoseconds (two-billionths of a second) per day, or one second in 1.4 million years. This is by far the greatest accuracy of any clock ever developed. Because of their great accuracy, atomic clocks are used to set International Atomic Time, the international standard time.

USING TIMEKEEPING DEVICES

Accurate timing devices are used in three different ways: to time a particular period (perhaps to boil an egg), as time switches (perhaps to turn the central heating on and off at certain times), and to measure how long an event takes, such as a race.

Period timers

Devices to time the cooking of food are in almost every home. Often they are a part of the stove. Sometimes they consist of a simple "countdown" timer. A period of 45 minutes, for example, is set on the timer, which then counts down to zero and rings a bell. These devices work like a mechanical clock, with gears and an escapement.

Other timers are electrical devices and use quartz crystals for accuracies of a few seconds a month. A simple digital timer may have a countdown display and sound an alarm at the end of the period. These timers may use batteries or main electricity.

Time switches

A simple device is used for keeping the lights in a stairwell switched on long enough for people to get upstairs. The lights stay on for a few minutes and then go off. The device is usually a pushbutton attached to a piston in a cylinder. Pushing on the button turns the light on and pushes the piston down the cylinder, expelling the air through a valve. The valve has a small hole in it that lets the air return to the cylinder slowly. This allows a spring to carry the piston and pushbutton back to their starting places, turning off the lights. This device is used to save electricity in large buildings.

◀ *Event timers are used at sporting events, and they display race times to spectators. Event timers usually are triggered automatically at the start and finish of a race, using electronic sensors at the start and finish lines. These sensors remove the delay that would be caused by a person keeping track of the time.*

Other time switches can be set to switch a device on and off once during a 24-hour period. More advanced switches have several on-and-off sequences, and some can be arranged to use the set sequences on certain days of the week.

A central-heating timer, for example, may be set to switch on from 6:00 AM until 10:00 AM and then from 4:00 PM until 11:00 PM. This would suit people who are out all day from Monday to Friday; but on Saturday and Sunday, when they may be at home all day, the timer might switch on the central heating at 7:00 AM and leave it on until 11:00 PM.

Sometimes, such a preset sequence is too rigid. Street lights, for example, need to be on for longer in winter than in summer. An electric, solar-dial time switch has a cam (a rotating, offset lobe) to gradually change the time settings through the year, taking into account the varying length of the night during the different seasons. The timer has a backup clockwork mechanism in case a power failure should throw the timing out. Each street light may also have a photoelectric cell (a device that converts sunlight into electrical energy) to switch it on if the light level falls dramatically during the day, perhaps during a storm.

Event timers

Timing the finals of the 100-meter sprint in the Olympics, for example, needs extremely accurate equipment and a way of starting and stopping the timer at the exact start and finish of the race.

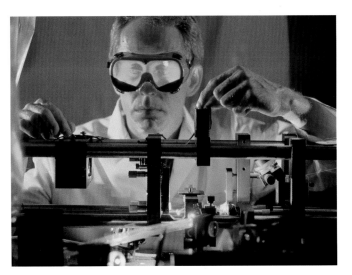

DID YOU KNOW?

A potentially new method of precise time measurement has recently been discovered by astronomers. This method would involve measuring the radio pulsations coming from collapsed stars, called pulsars. The periodic, and highly regular radio pulses caused by the pulsars' rapid rotation in their own magnetic field may provide accuracies that surpass those achievable with atomic clocks.

Times accurate to one-hundredth of a second are commonplace with quartz timers. The start of timing is triggered by a pulse of electricity from the starter's gun. The finish is timed by the winner breaking a light beam as he or she crosses the finishing line. A high-speed movie camera is also linked to the timing device, so the order of finishing and the times of each runner are photographed. The time of the winner is usually displayed on a board near the finish and eventually on the main display board, which also carries the names of all the runners and their times.

In case the device breaks down or fails to register either the start or the finish, there are a number of judges with ordinary stopwatches. Two or three judges time each runner and compare the times on their watches. Then all their times are compared with that of the timing device.

Some industrial and scientific processes also need the same sort of accuracy (or even greater) in their timing. If possible, the event being timed is arranged so it triggers the start and finish of the timing, as with the timing of a race. This keeps human error to a minimum.

◀ *Atomic clocks are the most accurate timekeeping devices yet created. Their complexity means that they are used only in specialized laboratories.*

See also: ASTRONOMY • ATOM AND MOLECULE • ELECTRIC MOTOR • PIEZOELECTRICITY • TIME

Tin

Tin is a soft, silvery metal that has been used as a component of alloys for more than four thousand years. Due to its low melting point, only a simple furnace is needed to melt the metal. Tin is one of the metals that makes bronze. It is also commonly used as a protective coating for other metals.

Tin does not rust, so one of its major uses is as a coating to protect other metals from corroding. Steel on its own, for example, soon rusts, but a tin coating prevents the steel from being eroded by oxygen. "Tin" cans—now often made of aluminum—were once made of tinplate, which is sheet steel coated with tin. Kitchen utensils are often electroplated with a thicker coating of tin. The protective coating of tin may be as little as $\frac{1}{25,000}$ inch (0.001 millimeter) thick.

In the metal industries, tin is mixed with other metals that have low melting points to make alloys. Bronze is an alloy of tin and copper. Tin and lead are mixed to make solder, which is used to join pipes. An alloy of tin and niobium is produced to make electrical wires. When mixed with either aluminum or copper, tin is used to make bearings in high-speed motors. Tin also forms a decorative alloy called pewter,

which used to be a common material for domestic utensils. The pewter was made with a high lead content, however, and the lead acted as a poison when used in plates and mugs. Pewter is now made from 92 percent tin, 6 percent antimony, and 2 percent copper.

Some glassmaking processes use tin; window glass is often produced by floating molten glass atop molten tin to make a flat surface. Tin is also a component of foil for wrapping food and drugs, although aluminum is also now preferred.

▶ Steel cans are coated with a thin layer of tin to protect the steel from rusting. Cans were invented in 1810 as a means of preserving food in an airtight container free from bacteria.

Tin used as a chemical

Tin compounds are used for a wide variety of purposes. A compound of tin and fluorine is present in some toothpaste. Tin chloride ($SnCl_2$) is also used in dyeing silk and weighting it (making it heavier) and in making perfumes. Tin can form compounds with carbon, which are used to make wood, paper, paint, textiles, agricultural sprays, and hospital disinfectants. Electronically conductive coatings are produced when tin salts are sprayed onto glass. These coatings are used in panel lighting and in the production of frost-free windshields. Tin oxides are made into pigments (coloring) for pottery. Faience and majolica, the colorful glazed potteries made several hundred years ago, were covered with a tin glaze before being fired.

Tin mining

Tin is one of the earliest metals to be mined by ancient peoples. Because of its hardening effect on copper, tin was used in bronze tools as far back as 3000 BCE, during a period of time known as the Bronze Age. Bronze had valuable uses in making not only tools and machinery, but also works of art. One of the first places where tin was mined was Cornwall, England. There is strong evidence of tin work in Cornwall from the early Bronze Age (2100–1500 BCE) and of a flourishing trade in tin with Mediterranean civilizations. However, pure tin was not produced until about 600 BCE.

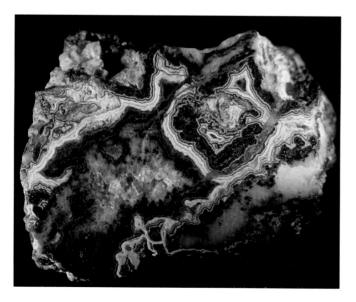

DID YOU KNOW?

Tin is a chemical element with the chemical symbol Sn and atomic number 50. Tin is harder than lead but softer than zinc. Its chemical symbol is derived from the Latin word for tin—*stannum*.

Tin is not found in its pure state but as part of other minerals (ores), mainly in cassiterite (tin oxide; SnO_2). Deposits of tin ores are concentrated in relatively few places throughout the world. The major tin producers are Bolivia, Brazil, China, Indonesia, and Malaysia. Other important producers include Argentina, Australia, Britain, Nigeria, Russia, South Africa, Thailand, and Zaire.

Extracting the tin

The principal tin ore, cassiterite, is widely scattered in a mine. Its host rock is usually granite but, in some places, weathering causes the mineral to be released as sand into streams. One ton of earth may yield just a few ounces of cassiterite, so the ore must be concentrated before smelting (melting down). It is crushed to a powder and roasted to remove impurities such as arsenic and sulfur.

To produce pure tin, the cassiterite is heated in a furnace with a form of coal called anthracite. The carbon in the coal combines with the oxygen in the cassiterite to form carbon dioxide gas. This escapes into the air, leaving the metallic tin behind. Sand is mixed with the cassiterite and anthracite to collect impurities from the metal. Sometimes tin has to be extracted from other metals, such as zinc and iron. Any tin that is not quite pure is sent for further processing. Tin is also refined through electrolysis. The refined product is called block tin.

◀ *This is a cut and polished section of a type of cassiterite called wood tin, so called because its banded structure has the appearance of wood. Wood tin occurs in igneous rocks such as granite.*

See also: ALLOY • METAL

Titanium

Titanium is one of the most versatile metals. It is both strong and light and has an extremely high melting point. Titanium is also resistant to corrosion. It is expensive to produce, however, so the widespread use of titanium is limited to a few specialist products.

Titanium (chemical symbol Ti) is as strong as some steels but has only half their weight. Titanium has a high melting point of 3034°F (1668°C). This is much higher than aluminum, another light metal. These properties make titanium an ideal material for high-tech applications such as supersonic aircraft because it can withstand the temperatures reached by airplanes traveling at very high speeds. In fact, titanium's properties make it so suitable as a building material for aircraft that it is often referred to as the aerospace metal. In practice, the titanium is often combined (alloyed) with other metals, such as vanadium or molybdenum, which improve its properties still further. As many airplanes get faster and faster, there will be a greater demand for titanium for the aircraft of the future.

Titanium reacts strongly with elements such as oxygen. This makes it resistant to corrosion (being attacked by the atmosphere or other chemicals). Once titanium has been exposed to oxygen, it combines with it to form a thin, tough layer of protective titanium oxide (TiO_2) on the surface of the metal. If this layer is scratched or scraped off, the titanium immediately recombines with oxygen to seal the damaged area.

Under and over water

Small seacraft are made using titanium. Racing yachts need strong, lightweight, flexible masts and spars; titanium is an ideal material. Titanium is also used on underwater craft because it can withstand the stresses of pressure and corrosion by seawater.

▲ The outside of the Guggenheim Museum in Bilbao, Spain, is clad with titanium panels. Titanium is an expensive construction material, but it is useful as it resists corrosion.

Power stations

When building power stations, design engineers look for materials that are durable and resistant to corrosion. Materials such as these are needed to build steam condensers in nuclear power stations. Steam condensers are made of hundreds of feet of metal piping and are used to cool the steam that drives the turbines in the power station. After the steam has been cooled so that it turns back into water, it is reused and heated up again inside the nuclear reactor.

Many power stations get the water for their steam cycles from the sea or from tidal rivers or estuaries. Within a few years, seawater corrodes even the strongest of alloys that have traditionally been used for condensers. This type of corrosion would produce dangerous leakages or contamination of the steam. Titanium is therefore the ideal material for condensers because it is so resistant to corrosion.

Spare parts

Titanium is not just resistant to corrosion by chemicals in the environment. It also resists the highly corrosive natural fluids produced by the human body. This means that titanium can be used to make the artificial joints that are implanted in certain types of surgery. For example, most replacement hip joints are made from titanium. Titanium is also ideal for making the tiny surgical instruments used by eye surgeons, especially because of the light weight of the metal. As a result, the surgeon can work longer without tiring and is better able to make the precise movements that are critical to eye surgery. Titanium also has long been used in bone screws, jaw implants, casings for heart pacemakers, and drug pumps that are implanted to give a person continuous medication.

Electrolytic refining and electroplating

Titanium has another valuable property. Unlike other metals, it does not corrode when a mild electrical current is passed through it. This means that it can be used in electroplating plants for heating coils, racks, and hooks in electrolysis units.

Copper refiners have also found a use for titanium in the electrolytic refining process. Titanium is used as the cathode (negative electrode) onto which thin layers of pure copper are deposited by electrolysis. This copper layer is then stripped from the cathode, and the copper is used as a new cathode on which larger quantities of high-purity solid copper are deposited during electrolysis. The advantages of using titanium first is that it does not contaminate the copper, and the thin copper layer pulls away easily and cleanly.

Titanium jewelry

Pure titanium is a silvery-gray metal. Although it will not corrode, it will change color dramatically when an electrical current is passed through it. By carefully adjusting the current, a whole range of shades can be produced. This makes titanium useful in jewelry making. The jeweler suspends the titanium in a tank containing an electrolyte (a liquid that will conduct electricity). When an electrical current is passed through the electrolyte, the surface of the metal changes color. Six volts produce a rich brown color. As the voltage increases, the color changes to purple, blue, and then to pale green. A further increase gives pink, purple, back through green to yellow, and finally, at 1,000 volts, pale pink. The only colors not produced are red and black.

◀ *These artificial hip implants are made from titanium. Titanium is an ideal material for this use because it is relatively light and strong, it resists corrosion, and it does not react with the body.*

Producing titanium

Titanium is the fourth most plentiful structural metal in Earth's crust after aluminum (Al), iron (Fe), and magnesium (Mg). However, titanium deposits rich enough to be worth extracting are not common. Commercial deposits of titanium are usually found as the ore minerals rutile (titanium dioxide; TiO_2) and ilmenite (iron-titanium oxide; $FeTiO_3$).

Most of the world's supply of titanium is produced from blackish-gray sands along the coastline of Eastern Australia. These sands are mined by huge dredgers that float in artificially excavated ponds on the beaches. The dredgers cut away massive sections of topsoil and then draw up the sands by suction. These machines can draw in as much as 1,500 tons (1,360 tonnes) of material in an hour. The material is piped to a concentration plant, which sifts the ore and leaves behind the unwanted silica sand.

Extracting and refining titanium ore is a difficult and expensive process. The extraction process involves treatment of the ore with chlorine gas (Cl_2) to produce titanium tetrachloride ($TiCl_4$), which is purified and reduced to a metallic titanium sponge by reaction with magnesium or sodium. The sponge is then refined through vacuum melting. A vacuum is required because titanium is so reactive, especially when melted, that it tries to combine with other elements such as oxygen, nitrogen, and hydrogen. All of these contaminate the metal and make it brittle.

The scarcity of viable deposits of titanium ore and the costly refining processes make titanium an expensive metal. Despite its valuable properties, these costs have restricted its widespread use.

See also: ELECTROLYSIS • ELECTROPLATING

Tool and tool manufacture

The ability to make and use tools is the fundamental advantage that has made the human race so successful. From buildings and automobiles to furniture and electrical goods, the human landscape has been shaped through the use of tools.

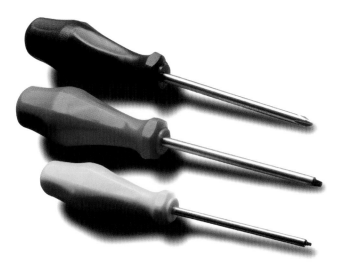

▲ *People have used simple hand tools for thousands of years. One of the most useful hand tools is the screwdriver, a relatively recent invention.*

In prehistoric times, as long as one million years ago, the early humans had already learned how to use simple tools to help them in their daily lives. For thousands of years, tools were made from stones that could be held in a person's hand. Flat stones with sharp edges were used as simple hand axes, and hard, round stones were used as hammers.

At the start of the Middle Stone Age, about 40,000 years ago, people started to make tools in two parts. They were made of more than one material, combined to add to the tool's power and usefulness. For example, many tools were hafted, that is, fitted with handles. The wood-hafted hand ax became a powerful tool with which people could cut down trees and clear the land. Early farmers in particular found this invaluable.

In the Middle Stone Age, the Mesolithic peoples started to use microliths, which are small flakes of flint rock, usually shaped in a triangle. Microliths were set into bone, wood, or horn to make many of the small tools of that age. The world's first farmers used microliths to make sickles, and builders used them to make saws. Using microliths made such tools last longer and saved a great deal of hard work for the toolmakers. If a flake fell off or got blunt, another one could be put in its place without having to make a whole new tool.

The Mesolithic peoples also improved on previous axes and adzes (an adze is a cutting tool with a blade set at right angles, used mostly for shaping wood). These tools had blades either of flint or of a rock such as chalcedony, which also produces flakes with sharp edges. The problem was that the long wooden handles could split easily because they already had holes bored into them for fitting the blade. The improvement was to set the blade in a sleeve made of bone or horn. This reduced some of the shock of a blow by spreading it over a wider area of the handle, which helped keep it from splitting.

In the Late Stone Age, the Neolithic peoples used the bow drill to bore holes in stone. A drill bit of hard wood was twisted into the bow string, and the bow was moved back and forth. This action made the bit spin and bite into the stone. Before using the bow drill, a pilot (guide) hole was pounded out with a hammer stone, and an abrasive for grinding and polishing was added. The bow drill and the abrasive wore away a hole. However, this hole was in the shape of a shallow dish, so another pilot had to be made from the other side. This is why holes in ancient objects are smaller and narrower in the middle than around the edges.

Metal tools

By about 4000 BCE, the first copper objects were being manufactured because the metal could now be smelted (made by melting down the metal-rich mineral, or ore). However, copper was scarce and proved too soft for toolmaking, so the metal was used only for making ornaments and weapons for people of importance. Tools such as the ax, adze, awl, hammer, saw, and sickle were all made of sharpened stones set in bone or horn sleeves, and they had wooden handles.

It was not until after the discovery of bronze (an alloy, or mixture, of copper and tin) around 3500 BCE that metal tools came into widespread use. After about 1500 BCE, iron began to replace bronze for making tools and weapons. By Roman times, blacksmiths had learned the secret of hardening and strengthening iron by heating it with charcoal.

Steel was first widely used for toolmaking after the invention of industrial steelmaking in Britain in the 1750s. Because of steel's great strength and resilience and its relatively low manufacturing cost, it has become the material from which practically all modern tools are made.

Casting, forging, and heat treating

Early metal objects made of copper and bronze were often cast. Casting involves pouring molten metal into shaped molds. When the metal has cooled and solidified, the mold is removed.

Until the development of the blast furnace about 1400 CE, iron could not be cast because furnaces could not be made hot enough to melt the metal properly. So iron tools had to be forged into shape by repeated hand hammering.

A great many modern tools, such as hammers and wrenches, are still forged rather than cast, but this is done by machines, such as drop forges, instead of by hand. Other modern tools, such as files and saws, are cut from steel bars or pressed from steel strips.

One important feature of metal tool manufacture is heat treatment and other finishing processes. During shaping operations such as forging, tool steel becomes stressed internally. These stresses could cause the metal to crack or make it otherwise unsuitable for use. So the metal is usually treated using heat to prevent this.

Heat-treatment processes include annealing and tempering. These treatments involve reheating the metal to a certain temperature. Then the metal may be cooled at a slow rate, or it may be plunged into cold water or oil so that it cools rapidly. Heat treatments increase the hardness, toughness, or springiness of the steel, depending on what properties are desired in the finished product.

The type of steel chosen for a particular tool varies widely. Ordinary saw blades are made from mild steel strip. High-speed drill bits, however, have to be made from high-carbon steels or special alloy steels. Such steels contain materials with high melting points, such as tungsten carbide (WC). These materials make the steel more heat resistant and allow it to run red-hot at high speeds and for long periods without softening.

TYPES OF SIMPLE TOOLS

Over the years, hundreds of different types of tools have evolved from working materials of every kind, from stone and wood to metal and plastic. Simple traditional tools, such as hammers and knives, have evolved, while new, complex, and specialized tools are continually being developed.

◀ One of the oldest tools is the handsaw. The Romans made the first significant development to the saw, inventing the angled teeth that are still used on many wood saws. Now there are many different handsaws for sawing timber, cutting joints, and even sawing through metal.

◄ *Power tools such as this cordless electric drill have removed much of the effort from many practical jobs. Power tools also have features that are not available on hand tools. This drill, for example, has a hammer action for drilling through masonry.*

The ancient Egyptians developed the saw, but it was the Romans who made it into an invaluable tool. They thought out the method of setting the teeth—bending them alternately to one side, then the other. This makes less sawdust and also leaves a wider slot in which the saw can travel.

Two basic wood saws are the cross-cut saw and the rip saw. These saws differ in the type of teeth they have. The cross-cut saw cuts best across the wood grain, while the rip saw cuts best with the grain. Other saws include the fine-toothed tenon saw for cutting joints, and the hacksaw, which has a narrow blade held in tension by a G-shaped frame and is widely used for metalwork.

A chisel is a metal tool with a sharpened edge at one end used to chip, carve, or cut into a solid material. Wood chisels have a flat blade with a sharp beveled cutting edge at the end. Cold chisels, used for cutting metal, have a rounded body and a flattened end. A bricklayer's chisel, called a bolster, has a broad cutting blade for cutting bricks.

Hammers

A hammer is classified as a percussive (striking) tool. It has a tempered steel head and a shaft. The shaft is usually made of a wood such as ash, though hardened metal tubing and plastic reinforced with fiberglass are also used. The hammer head is fastened to the shaft by means of wedges.

Different types of hammers have been developed for various purposes. Among the most common is the carpenter's claw hammer. This has a two-pronged claw at the top, opposite the striking face, which is used to pull nails out of wood. A ball-peen hammer has a rounded top, while a cross-peen hammer has a wedge-shaped top. Some hammer-like tools have a striking face of rubber, wood, or leather, and they are usually called mallets.

Cutting tools

The oldest cutting tool is the knife, and certain craft workers, such as woodcarvers and leatherworkers, still use special knives in their work. The most useful general-purpose cutting tools, however, are saws and chisels.

Screwdrivers

One of the most useful tools is the screwdriver. Screws first appeared in the fifteenth century as more effective fasteners than nails. Screws are available for use with wood or metal and come in many shapes and sizes. Most screws have one of two types of head: either slotted or cross-cut (Phillips). Flat-blade screwdrivers are used for slotted screws, and cross-head screwdrivers are used for cross-cut screws. Screwdrivers are available with different sized heads to fit different sized screws. The shanks of screwdrivers are made of tough steel, and the tips are hardened to minimize wear.

Smoothing tools

The tool most often used for smoothing a rough surface or for cutting a thin piece of wood is the plane. This tool was first used by the Romans. It has an angled blade with a sharp cutting edge at the bottom that projects through a slot in the base of the plane. When the plane is pushed forward, the blade cuts a thin piece of wood.

A spokeshave or drawknife is a simple planing device consisting of a narrow cutting blade held between two handles. A modern kind of plane, called the surform plane, has a cutting surface composed of sharp metal mesh. Files also have a multitoothed cutting edge. They are available in many kinds of cross-sectional shapes, including flat, round, half-moon, triangular, and square.

POWER TOOLS

Soon after the widespread generation and national distribution of electricity, many tools became motorized, taking advantage of electric motors to make their operation easier and faster. Handheld electrical tools, called power tools, became widely available from the 1950s. Power tools include electric drills, polishers, sanders, saws, screwdrivers, and many more devices that are continually being developed for the construction industry and the home-improvement market.

The development of long-lasting, powerful, and rechargeable batteries in the 1990s allowed many power tools to become portable, or cordless, making them more useful. Once the tools' battery packs are drained, they can be recharged from the main electricity supply and reused many times.

Although most power tools are driven by electricity, tools such as impact wrenches and hammers are driven by compressed air. These are called pneumatic tools.

MACHINE TOOLS

A machine tool works by electricity and is used to cut or shape metal. Drill presses, lathes, and milling machines are machine tools. Some of them, especially lathes and milling machines, can work in many different ways, and they are often automatic.

▶ *This machinist is using a computer-controlled metal lathe to shape a piece of copper. Metal lathes are machine tools, that is, machines that can be used to make parts for other machines.*

Machine tools are essential in modern industries that make large quantities of metal parts. They are used to produce parts for many other machines, such as automobiles and airplanes, and they are also capable of reproducing themselves. There are several types of machine tools, and they are used for shaping, planing, drilling, milling, and grinding.

Lathes

Lathes are the most common type of machine tool, as well as the oldest and one of the most important. A lathe is used to shape a piece of wood or metal (the workpiece) by clamping the object and rotating it at high speed.

The principle of the lathe has been known since ancient times. The idea was probably suggested by the potter's wheel. Early lathes were used to make wooden spindles, chair legs, and other rounded wooden objects. By the eighteenth century, soft metals were being shaped on lathes. By the nineteenth century, rapid advances in lathe building occurred because accurate parts were needed for the new textile machinery and steam engines of the Industrial Revolution.

The lathe is probably the most useful metal-cutting machine. It is extremely accurate and can perform cutting or shaping operations to within

$^1/_{10,000}$ inch (0.0002 centimeter). The advantage of the lathe is that by directing the tool at various angles, almost any type of shape is possible.

How the lathe works

The workpiece is fixed in the revolving chuck (clamp) of the lathe. A tool can be moved onto the face of the workpiece. If the tool is moved along the axis of spin, a hole will be drilled in the center of the workpiece. If the tool is applied away from the axis of spin, a circular section will be cut out of the workpiece. By combining these two motions and working at different angles, metal parts of all shapes and sizes can be produced. These can be a simple screw or a complicated engine crankshaft.

In most lathes, the workpiece is rotated on a horizontal axis, and it usually needs support at both ends. The support at one end rotates the workpiece. This is called the headstock. The support at the other end is the tailstock. They are mounted on a flat bed, but the tailstock is adjustable to match the length of the workpiece. Mounted on the bed is a metal rail or guide, along which the tool carriage slides. This carriage holds the tool firmly and may feed it toward the workpiece automatically. The tools may be lubricated with a constant stream of oil to keep them from overheating.

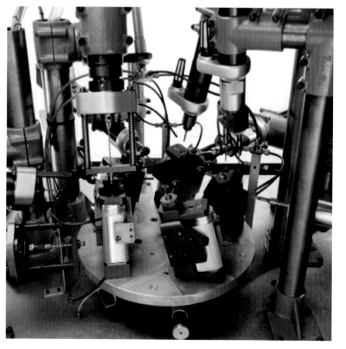

Shapers and planers

Shaping and planing tools are used for working on the surface of pieces of metal. They are known as reciprocating machine tools because they contain parts that move back and forth.

In a shaper, the cutting tools are at the end of a ram that moves back and forth. The workpiece is fixed to a work table. As the ram moves forward, the tool cuts into the surface of the workpiece. As the ram moves back, the tool returns along the same path. At the end of each cycle (one forward and backward movement of the ram), the table holding the workpiece is moved sideways. In this way the tool cuts a new strip of metal from the workpiece on the next forward stroke. The height of the work table can be adjusted so that the metal is cut to the right depth. The length of the ram stroke can be adjusted to suit the length of the workpiece.

Some shapers work by another method. The ram is driven by a hydraulic piston operated by a pump that automatically changes its speed between the forward and return strokes.

A planing machine works in a similar way to a shaper. In this case, however, the cutting tool remains fixed, while the table that holds the workpiece moves back and forth.

Milling machines

Shapers, planers, and lathes use single-bladed tools that remain in the same position as they cut. A typical milling machine, on the other hand, has a tool with several blades, rotating on a spindle. The tool is lowered onto the metal workpiece, which is fixed to a sliding table. The workpiece is cut by each blade in turn as the tool spins.

There are two kinds of milling machines: those with horizontal spindles and those with vertical spindles. In a machine with a horizontal spindle, the tool is usually round and flat, with the blades at the edge, similar to the blade of a circular saw. The

◀ *This small milling machine comprises a number of drills set at different angles. It is used to drill complex sets of holes and channels in machine parts. Some large milling machines can be the size of a room.*

◄ **Many manufacturers use specialized tools. In this picture, a worker assembles a utility knife using a bench tool manufactured specifically for the task.**

instead of spiral ones. A drill press can also be used to tap a hole, which means to cut a thread inside the hole so that a bolt can be inserted.

Honing and grinding

A hone is used to enlarge or finish a hole to an exact size, such as a cylinder bore in an engine block. It is a cylindrical tool with a rotating abrasive tip.

Grinding machines are used to polish metal surfaces or to reduce them to precise sizes. To grind a flat surface, a grinding wheel is lowered from above onto the workpiece, which is fixed to a movable table. The workpiece turns somewhat slowly, while the grinding wheel rotates against it at high speed in the opposite direction.

Computerized machine tools

The computer, as well as the development of robotics and hydraulics, has revolutionized the use of many machine tools. Modern machine tools need less attention from their operators, and they work with greater precision.

When a number of identical parts are to be produced, the machine tool can be programmed to repeat a certain pattern. All the operator has to do is take out the finished piece and put in a fresh blank after each pass of the tool.

Frequently, a series of machining operations must be carried out on a number of identical parts. In such cases, machine tools are arranged either in a circle or in a straight line, and the components are transferred automatically from one machine to the next. Many machine tools have digital readout devices that show the operator the changing size of the workpiece as it is being cut. Others are controlled by computers programmed to make the machine perform a number of different operations, one after the other.

tool is lowered onto the workpiece to cut channels into the metal. A machine with a vertical spindle has a tool known as an end mill, with spiral cutting edges. An end mill can be used to cut slots and large holes.

Modern milling machines can perform many different tasks. By using certain cutters, complex machining can contour the surface of a piece of metal. If the workpiece is mounted on a movable head, a milling machine can cut elaborately shaped holes or spiral channels.

Drill presses

The simplest drill press is an ordinary electric hand drill clamped onto a vertical column. The drill can be moved up and down by means of a rack and pinion gear. An industrial drill press is similar. An electric motor operates a spindle on which various sized drills can be attached. The workpiece is clamped to a table below the spindle.

For drilling holes that need to be an exact size, a small drill is used first. Then the hole is widened by a reamer, which has straight flutes (channels)

See also: BLAST FURNACE • DRILL • HYDRAULICS • IRON AND STEEL • ROBOTICS

Tornado

Tornadoes are small but destructive storms. They are also called twisters. In the centers of tornadoes, the winds are so strong that trees are uprooted, trains are blown off their tracks, and animals and even people have been lifted high above the ground.

The causes of tornadoes are not fully understood. Like tropical cyclones (hurricanes), they are whirling masses of air. While hurricanes are usually 125 to 250 miles (200 to 400 kilometers) across, tornadoes are small in size and seldom measure more than about 867 yards (790 meters) across. Despite their size, tornadoes can cause more destruction than hurricanes.

A tornado resembles a long, funnel-shaped tube of cloud, which extends downward from the bottom of a dark cumulonimbus (thunderstorm) cloud. At ground level, moist air is drawn horizontally into the tube. Within the tube, air is drawn upward in a spiral at speeds of 200 miles (320 kilometers) per hour or more. Wind speeds may well reach twice this speed inside a tornado. No one knows for sure because the instruments that measure wind speeds are always destroyed when a tornado passes over them.

The whirling air creates a roaring sound, which gets increasingly louder as the tornado approaches. People who hear this roar should quickly seek shelter in some low place because tornadoes can be extremely dangerous. The roofs of houses are often blown off by the rapidly spiraling air, and people have been known to be scooped up to heights of hundreds of feet before falling back to the ground. The updraft in the heart of a tornado is often so intense that steel bridges are pulled from their foundations. Sometimes the bottom of a tornado leaves the ground, and the devastation at ground level stops.

▲ *This photograph shows a tornado that occurred in Kansas in 2004. The spinning column of air stretches from the clouds to the ground, sucking up objects in its path.*

In areas where air rises, the air pressure falls quickly. The air pressure in a tornado may be only one-tenth of the average air pressure at sea level. The low air pressure and cool air cause invisible water vapor in the air to condense into a mass of tiny, visible water droplets, making the funnel that snakes down from the cumulonimbus cloud clearly visible.

The low pressure is also responsible, together with the high wind speeds, for the damage to property. The air pressure inside buildings remains normal and is, therefore, so different from the air pressure in the tornado that the walls and windows of buildings sometimes blow out as the tornado passes around them. After the tornado has moved on, the shattered buildings look as though they have been deliberately blown up by explosives.

Where tornadoes occur

One part of the world is affected by tornadoes more than any other: the American Midwest, especially Kansas and Oklahoma, an area that is sometimes called "tornado alley." Between March and June, warm, moist air flows northward from the Gulf of Mexico into the Midwest, while cold, dry air from the north flows over it. This air flow causes strong upward air currents to form. As the lower air rises and its water vapor condenses, heat contained in the air is released, which speeds up the rising air currents. The water droplets develop into massive cumulonimbus clouds, and thunder and heavy rain often occur.

In the right conditions, tornadoes also develop, and sometimes several tornadoes appear on the same day. Tornadoes travel in roughly straight lines at 6 to 40 miles (10 to 65 kilometers) an hour. Many die out after 20 miles (32 kilometers), but others can travel up to 300 miles (485 kilometers), leaving a narrow trail of destruction behind them.

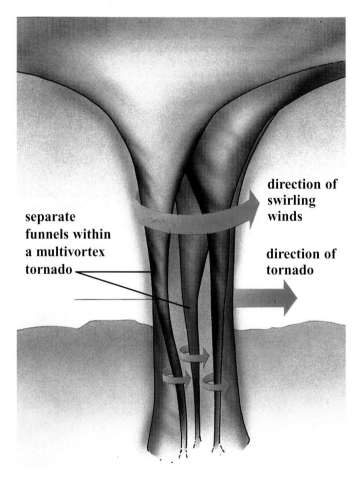

separate funnels within a multivortex tornado

direction of swirling winds

direction of tornado

▲ This illustration shows the movement of a tornado that contains more than one funnel (a multivortex tornado). The smaller, inner funnels spin rapidly around at the same time as the main exterior funnel.

On average, 500 to 600 tornadoes occur every year in the United States, although the amount of damage they cause depends on their path.

One of the most destructive tornadoes of all time occurred in the south-central United States on March 18, 1925. In three hours, it killed 689 people. During 16 hours of April 1974, 148 tornadoes swept through 11 states, leaving 314 people dead and 6,000 injured and destroying property valued at $600 million. Tornadoes occur in other countries, such as Australia, but they are less common and generally less destructive. Between 1963 and 1966, tornadoes occurred in Britain on a total of 36 days, but damage was mostly slight.

Waterspouts

Waterspouts are similar to tornadoes, but they occur over large bodies of water. Like tornadoes, waterspouts usually start when a funnel-shaped cloud descends from a cumulonimbus cloud down to a water surface. Water is then drawn up by the warm, spiraling air.

Waterspouts have been known to capsize small boats and rip away their masts and sails. They have also washed sailors overboard and have even caused damage to large ocean liners. Often, the tops of waterspouts, which may be several hundred feet high, move faster than the base. Eventually, the waterspout bends so much that it breaks and disappears. Waterspouts usually travel slowly, and they die out soon after they reach land. Waterspouts occur more often in tropical and subtropical seas than seas at high latitudes.

See *also:* AIR • PRESSURE • RAIN AND RAINFALL

Touch

Without the sense of touch, it would be hard to tell if objects were real or simply imagined. Touch also gives people the ability to feel pain, which helps them avoid harmful situations.

The sense of touch is an invaluable way of understanding the world. It is useful when assessing objects and situations and can also help indicate people's feelings. Unlike the other senses of sight, hearing, smell, and taste, touch is not limited to one part of the body but can be felt over the whole surface area (the skin).

Touch allows people to respond to both temperature and pressure. It helps people feel the shape, size, and texture of things—whether they are hard or soft, hot or cold, rough or smooth—and whether they cause pain. It gives useful warning signals. For example, a flame is felt as both heat and pain. Having experienced the pain, a person is unlikely to thrust a hand into a fire.

Although skin all over the body is capable of feeling, some areas are more sensitive than others. The tips of the tongue, nose, and fingers are particularly responsive to touch, and the backs of the shoulders are least sensitive. This difference occurs because the nerves in the skin that respond to touch are more highly concentrated in some parts of the body than in others.

These nerves are similar to threads or fibers and connect the surface of the body to the brain. Each differently shaped receptor (nerve ending) is responsive to one or more kind of touch. Scientists have found that some types of nerves are particularly sensitive to light touch (Meissner corpuscles); others respond to heavier pressure (Pacinian corpuscles). Some nerves are responsive to cold (Krausse end bulbs) and others to heat (Ruffini corpuscles). The nerve endings without any particular shape are sensitive to pain.

▲ **This blind person is reading by touch using Braille. Characters are formed with "cells" of six dots, arranged in two columns. Each dot can be raised, giving 64 different combinations. These form letters and punctuation marks.**

Messages to the brain

Once receptors have picked up sensations on the skin, the information is sent along nerve fibers to the brain, which processes the information. If a person dips his or her toes into cold water, for example, he or she will recognize cold and discomfort and may decide not to go for a swim after all.

Nerve fibers vary in thickness, which affects the speed at which messages travel to the brain. If these fibers become damaged through disease, the brain will not receive messages from the skin, and a person may then appear to have no sense of touch.

Just as some people have particularly good hearing, some individuals experience stronger sensations of touch than others. Blind people often

▶ *The many receptors in the human skin respond to sensations of pressure, pain, heat, and cold and send information about these to the brain. Free nerve endings respond to pain, Krausse end bulbs respond to cold, and Ruffini corpuscles respond to heat. The cross section of the skin shown in this illustration reveals that most of these receptors are situated in the bottom layer, called the dermis.*

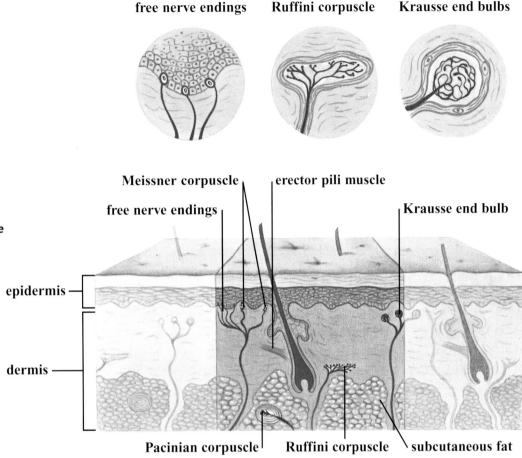

free nerve endings **Ruffini corpuscle** **Krausse end bulbs**

Meissner corpuscle   erector pili muscle

free nerve endings   Krausse end bulb

epidermis

dermis

Pacinian corpuscle   Ruffini corpuscle   subcutaneous fat

develop a special sensitivity to touch, which helps them recognize objects they cannot see. The Braille system was invented in 1829 to allow the blind to "read." Words are translated into a code of raised dots on a page. These can be recognized by sensitive fingertips. Children taught Braille from a young age are able to read it at approximately the same speed as sighted children can read words.

The degree of pain that can be tolerated also varies between individuals. In fact, pain can be deceptive. For example, some mothers experience childbirth as extremely painful and require pain relief, whereas others seem to cope much better and can give birth without taking painkillers. It has also been found that people who have had an arm or leg cut off still experience painful sensations when they no longer have the limb.

The feeling of pain can be affected by cultural factors, too. Some societies, for example, require young people to undergo painful procedures bravely before they are considered to be adults.

Human contact

How well people get along with each other depends partly on the amount of physical contact they have and what form it takes. Touching is often a sign of affection. This includes hugging, kissing, stroking, and even friendly pats on the back. People choose to have more contact with people they like and stand closer to family members and friends than to strangers, when close contact may feel uncomfortable.

Infants need to come into close contact with their parents so they feel loved and reassured. Scientists have found that infants who have been deprived of this contact (perhaps because they had to have special treatment in a hospital immediately after birth) suffer later in life. They tend not to make friends as easily as children who have experienced physical tenderness from birth.

See also: ANESTHETIC • BRAIN • CELL • EYE AND VISION • SKIN • SMELL • TASTE

Traffic control

During the last few decades, the volume of traffic has increased greatly. All this traffic has to be carefully controlled; otherwise, the streets of cities and towns will become blocked. Many traffic signals are needed.

Many towns and cities in the world were built long before the automobile was invented. Their streets were not made to handle large numbers of motorized vehicles. Now that there are so many automobiles and trucks on the streets, traveling can be difficult. The main streets of cities and towns become congested (blocked up with traffic), and this causes many problems.

One problem is that trips take much longer because heavy traffic moves so slowly. Also, more fuel is used when drivers have to stop and start their cars all the time. Often, drivers in a traffic jam become impatient. They turn off the main street and use side streets that are unsuitable for heavy traffic. This increases the traffic's impact on the environment. Vibrations caused by moving vehicles damage buildings, and exhaust fumes from vehicles poison the atmosphere.

Building new roads

At first, town planners thought that the answer to congestion was to build more roads. As a result, multilane highways were constructed. These roads do help cut down the congestion in towns because a lot of traffic bypasses the towns altogether.

If there are too many highways, however, the environment suffers. If more roads lead to a town, more traffic goes through it. Also, there is a limit to the number of roads that can be built. Other ways of controlling the amount traffic have to be found.

Public-transportation networks can be expanded and improved so that they offer reliable, flexible, and less expensive alternatives to driving. Increased vehicle, fuel, and road taxes may also discourage people from driving.

For the many millions of vehicles remaining on the roads, effective traffic controls are essential to avoid chaos and ensure that traffic flow is as efficient as possible.

▶ *The complex network of roads, overpasses, and bridges in this picture illustrates the difficulties of managing the large volumes of traffic found in and around major urban centers.*

◄ *Traffic control is particularly important in busy cities, where there are multiple road users. As well as automobiles and trucks, there can also be pedestrians, cyclists, motorcyclists, buses, and streetcars to control.*

Traffic signals and signs

There have been traffic signals and signs for as long as there has been traffic. In the early twentieth century, the Wayne County Road Commission, Michigan, started using white lines down the center of the roads to separate driving lanes. In the early 1920s, Detroit introduced automatic traffic signals. In present-day New York City, there are nearly one million traffic signals.

Early traffic signals were controlled locally, by preset switches in boxes at the side of the signals, or by pads in the road over which vehicle wheels passed. However, separate controls for each set of signals result in much stopping and starting. It is much more efficient to coordinate all the signals in an area using an area traffic control system. This system works by linking all the signals to a central computer. Most traffic signaling throughout the world operates through some type of area traffic control. There are several different systems.

TRANSYT

The TRANSYT system is used in many countries. With the TRANSYT system, all the signals in an area are on time switches. Their timing is changed for different periods of the day or week because the amount of traffic varies. For example, there is far more congestion in the rush hour on a weekday than there is over a weekend.

The time switches are coordinated so that, if possible, once traffic has been allowed through one set of signals, it will not have to stop again. This is called a green wave. In practice, green waves seldom occur. It is difficult to make them work in both directions on a two-way road. Also, traffic spreads out unevenly between intersections (where roads cross). Making allowances for this is problematic.

SCOOT

In the split-cycle-and-off-set-optimizing technique (SCOOT) system, the timing of the signals changes according to how much traffic there is on the streets and what it is doing. The flow of traffic is measured by a number of detectors buried in the road. The detectors are wire loops that generate a magnetic field. When a vehicle passes over a detector, the magnetic field is disturbed. A pulse (signal) then passes back to the central computer. The detectors can provide information about the flow and volume of traffic and traffic jams.

Traffic controllers at a central office watch over the system, which is displayed on large screens. If a set of signals fails, or if there is an accident that stops the flow of traffic, the controllers know immediately and can take action. If emergency services are needed, the controller can send the fire engine or ambulance along a set route and ensure that all the signals are green.

Traffic and pedestrians

Signals for pedestrians are computerized, too. A pedestrian wanting to cross the road can press a switch in a box at the side of the road to change the signals. A sign on the other side of the road tells the pedestrian when the traffic lights have turned red.

Traffic control on highways

Express highways—such as turnpikes, freeways, thruways, and expressways—have no intersections or stoplights, and few junctions (meetings with other highways) do. However, the traffic does move at high speeds.

Control on most express highways is achieved using signs. These may be mounted over the highway or at the side of the road. In addition to identification of the various exits and junctions,

signs warn of areas subject to hazards from certain weather conditions. Some state and interstate highways display electronic signs, which warn drivers of various problems, such as accidents, fog, ice, and so on. Some signs will even add such instructions as to reduce speed.

Control of cars entering express highways is also being tried in certain areas with systems of ramp metering. In one such system, a red light on an entrance ramp holds a vehicle until there is a gap in the traffic in the lane into which the vehicle will enter. Then the traffic signal changes to green, and the vehicle is allowed onto the highway. In another system, the amount of traffic approaching the point where the ramp joins the highway is measured, as is the space beyond the merge. This tells how much more traffic can fit onto the road, and the traffic lights signal accordingly. Ramp control systems can increase travel speeds while reducing accidents.

Travel news

About 25 percent of highway accidents are caused by other (often quite small) accidents. For example, if two automobiles stop or slow down because they have hit or sideswiped each other, several more vehicles may collide with them.

◀ *In many countries, speed cameras are used to control speeding vehicles. Speed cameras measure the speed of a vehicle as it passes. If the vehicle is traveling faster than the speed limit, a photograph is taken of the vehicle's license plate, and a fine is sent to the owner. The driver may also gain points on his or her license, and too many points may lead to a driving suspension.*

▲ *Area traffic control centers such as the one shown constantly monitor traffic conditions and control road signals to minimize congestion.*

One way of solving this problem is to broadcast news about traffic delays due to road works, accidents, and floods over the radio. These broadcasts are made on FM radio channels using the radio data system (RDS). Each message starts with a special code, which blocks out other stations on RDS-equipped vehicle radios while the traffic message is being broadcast.

An idea in development is advance warning equipment (AWARE). In this system, each vehicle would have a visual display unit (screen) on the dashboard. Warning messages would be transmitted by way of wire loops buried in the road, and the signals would be displayed on the screen.

Often journeys take longer because drivers do not know the best route. In North America, Europe, and some other parts of the world, automatic route-guidance systems have been developed. These systems rely on the satellite-based Global Positioning System (GPS). A GPS device in the vehicle constantly monitors its position on the ground and compares this information with pre-programmed route information. The driver can enter a destination into the unit and then be guided to his or her destination by audible directions and a route displayed on a screen.

Restricting traffic

Traffic signals are only one part of traffic control. It is also necessary to have rules about where traffic can and cannot go. One-way streets, parking lots, parking meters, and special bus lanes all help to keep streets clear for through traffic.

Certain areas might benefit from even more restrictions. In very congested city centers, for example, it is possible to charge drivers for entering the area. This is done by metering. Wire loops in the road mark the metering points and send signals to closed meters in the vehicles; or curbside equipment monitors vehicles and gives the information to a central computer. This sort of traffic control has become more common as the amount of traffic in towns and cities increases.

See also: AUTOMOBILE • ROAD AND ROAD CONSTRUCTION

Transducer

A transducer is an instrument that changes one form of energy into another. The microphone, for example, changes the kinetic energy of sound waves into electrical energy. The loudspeaker changes electrical energy back into sound. Other transducers change movement into an electrical signal so it can be read on a meter.

Transducers are widely used in many electrical devices, particularly as parts of measuring instruments. Transducers are usually composed of two different parts. One part of the transducer measures a movement of some kind, while the other part changes the measured movement into an electrical signal. An example of this kind of transducer is an automobile fuel gauge.

The fuel gauge is an instrument mounted on the dashboard of an automobile. It tells the driver how much gasoline is in the tank. The transducer is attached to the fuel tank. It is called a displacement transducer because it measures the displacement of liquids and gases, that is, their movement from one place to another. A float goes into the fuel tank and moves up and down with the level of the fuel in the tank. Connected to the float is a potentiometer, which changes the movement of the float into an electrical signal. The signal is sent along a wire to the fuel gauge on the dashboard.

The whole operation of measuring displacement and changing it to electrical signals through a potentiometer gives the fuel gauge the full name of potentiometric transducer.

▼ *This microscopic image shows a micromechanical friction transducer. Lines of interlocking teeth are drawn together with the application of an electrical current, slowing the movable bar at the center.*

Inductive transducers

There are drawbacks to using potentiometric transducers, mainly because they make use of a moving contact. This can be affected by dirt, shaking, or the rubbing of the moving parts. To avoid these problems, there are transducers that do not use contact as part of the instrument. They rely instead on induction. Induction occurs when the changing magnetic field due to currents flowing in one object creates currents with their own magnetic field in a second object.

An example of this type of transducer is the linear variable differential transformer (LVDT). Its main parts are an E-shaped magnetic core and an I-shaped armature. Each of the three bars of the "E" has a coil of wire wound around it. The two outer coils are connected to an alternating current (AC) electricity supply. The center coil produces an output voltage. The "I" bar is set near the three bars of the "E" and is placed so that it either moves back and forth or up and down with the machinery to which it is attached, or so that it rotates on turning machinery.

▲ *Loudspeakers are transducers. The part of the speaker that converts electrical into mechanical energy is called the motor, or voice coil. This vibrates a diaphragm that, in turn, vibrates the air in contact with it, producing a sound wave corresponding to the original signal.*

DID YOU KNOW?

Weather data is gathered and sent to ground stations using a sensor and transducer system called a radiosonde. The sensors and transmitting elements are attached to weather balloons, and they measure temperature, pressure, and humidity.

With the "I" bar stationary, the magnetic fields generated by the two outer "E" bars are received by the "I" bar and transmitted to the center "E" bar, where they are canceled out with no output from the center bar. If the machinery to which the bar is fixed moves, this balance is upset. Instead of canceling out, the center bar produces a voltage of varying strength, according to how much or how little the bar is displaced. This type of transducer is used in industry to measure the movement of machine parts.

Other transducers

The capacitive transducer works by using the properties of a capacitor, which can store electrical charges. Capacitors have two electrically conductive plates separated by a piece of nonconducting material, such as mica. Any changes in any of the parts will mean a change in the capacitance, or potential charge stored, which can be picked up and made to register on a meter or gauge.

Strain gauges are transducers for measuring the strain of materials and various structures. The main part of the gauge is a piece of wire that has electrical resistance. When the wire is stretched, it becomes longer and thinner, and the resistance will also increase according to how much strain is put on it. By measuring the electrical resistance of the wire, the amount of strain can also be measured.

See also: CAPACITOR • INDUCTION • RESISTANCE • TRANSFORMER

Transformer

A transformer is an electrical device that is used to raise or lower voltage. It transfers electrical power between two electric circuits with alternating current at different voltages. Power from main electricity cables is reduced through transformers for distribution to factories and homes.

A simple transformer consists of two electrical windings around the same magnetic circuit. When an alternating current (AC) is applied to the primary winding, an AC current flows. The voltage of this current is limited by inductance. Inductance is the property of a conductor or circuit that, when an electrical current flows through it, causes a magnetic field to be set up around it.

This magnetizing current produces an alternating magnetomotive force that creates an alternating magnetic flux (flow). The magnetic flux cannot escape the magnetic circuit, and it induces a voltage in the secondary winding. The secondary winding will produce an AC current when it is connected to an electrical load.

In turn, the secondary load current produces its own magnetomotive force. This force creates a further alternating flux and then links back to the primary winding. A load current then flows in the primary winding, which is strong enough to balance the magnetomotive force produced by the secondary load current.

So the primary winding carries both magnetizing and load current. The secondary winding carries load current, and the magnetic circuit carries only the flux produced by the magnetizing current.

Voltage ratios

The voltages across each winding and the currents flowing in them are related to each other by the ratio of the number of turns in the two windings. If the primary winding has N_1 turns and the secondary winding has N_2 turns, the primary and secondary voltages (V_1 and V_2) can be related using the following formula:

$$V_1 \div V_2 = N_1 \div N_2$$

and the currents (I_1 and I_2) by:

$$I_1 \div I_2 = N_2 \div N_1$$

◄ *Electricity is sent through the national grid at high current to help minimize loss. Transformers (the large square-shaped object shown at the left of this picture) are used in substations to reduce this high current to a level suitable for home or commercial supply.*

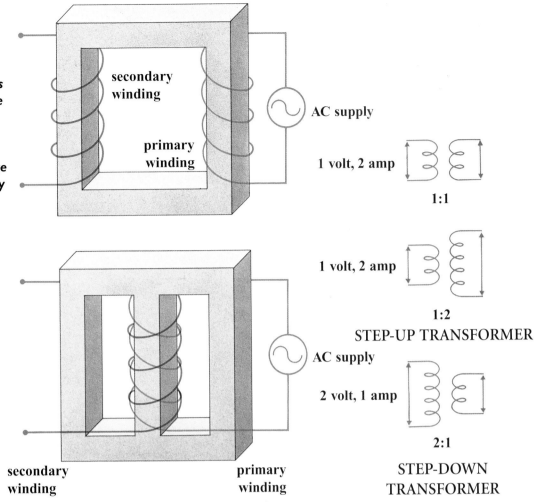

▶ *These illustrations show the two main winding arrangements for transformers with solid cores. The windings may appear on separate limbs (top), or together on one central limb (bottom). The winding conductors must be large enough to withstand any mechanical force to which the transformer may be subjected.*

When a transformer is used to transfer power between two electric circuits operating at different voltages, the currents flowing in each winding are in inverse (opposite) ratio to the voltages.

Transformer design

The magnetic circuit, called the core, is made from steel—usually alloyed (mixed) with silicon. This reduces the reluctance (ratio of magnetic resistance offered by a magnetic circuit to the passage of magnetic flux) of the flux path and gives a low magnetizing current. The core is made up of thin steel laminations (layers) that are insulated from each other. If the core was solid, it would act as a shorted turn, enclosing the flux path. This would permit a circulating current to flow, producing a high eddy current loss. The windings are made of a material with a low resistivity, such as copper or aluminum in strip form.

The importance of insulation

The electrical insulation of the windings is very important. The conductor turns must be insulated from each other, and there must also be enough insulation between the windings and from each winding to earth. This must be enough to withstand any exceptionally large voltages that may occur, for example, through lightning strikes.

Common insulating materials include paper, wood, and mineral oil. Each of these must be as free of water as possible, or their insulating properties will be considerably reduced. Air-cooled transformers are usually made with high-temperature inorganic insulating materials. They may be treated with resin or silicone varnish to prevent water from seeping in.

See also: ELECTRICITY • INDUCTION • INSULATOR • MAGNETISM • TESLA COIL

Transistor

A transistor is a device in which the voltage in one part of a circuit can control the resistance to current flow in another. They are widely used as amplifiers to make signals stronger in many devices and as switches in computer circuits.

A transistor is a semiconductor device—it is made from a material that does not conduct electricity well enough to be called a conductor or badly enough to be called an insulator.

Until 1948, electron tubes were used to amplify (increase) electrical signals and also to generate fast oscillations (changes in the direction of an alternating current; AC) that are needed in electronic systems. Later, a device called a germanium point contact transistor was developed that could amplify and oscillate without needing to be heated like electron tubes. Much work has been done to develop this instrument, and the present-day space-saving and power-saving transistor is the result of this work.

Semiconductors

To understand how the transistor works, it is necessary to understand something about the semiconducting material from which it is made.

Semiconductors are crystals of compounds containing elements such as germanium, selenium, and silicon. In these materials, a few electrons break free from the outer shells of the atoms at normal temperatures. Even a small electrical field causes these electrons to move toward the positive terminal (connection) of the power source. When the electrons break free from the outer shells of the atoms, they leave spaces, or "holes." When electrons flow toward a positive electrical pole, it is called n-type conductivity. The holes behave in the opposite way, like positive electrons, conducting free neighboring electrons. This causes a secondary, indirect movement called p-type conductivity.

The pn junction

Semiconductor crystals can be made to increase their conduction by adding other substances, which act as impurities in a process called doping. If an impurity, such as indium or arsenic, is added to a pure germanium crystal, then extra free-moving electrons are created, and the germanium becomes n type. This is because both indium and arsenic have five electrons in their outer shells, whereas germanium has only four. When the electrons pair up, there is one left over. To make p-type germanium, gallium or antimony can be added as an impurity. These have only three electrons in their outer shell. The space where another negative electron should be is a positively charged hole.

One end of the crystal can be doped with an impurity that makes it n type, and the other end with a different impurity, making it a p type. The middle section, where the two types meet, is called an pn junction.

When the n-type end is connected to the negative terminal of a battery, and the p-type end to the positive terminal, electrons will move from the n-type side, across the junction, to the positive connection. Meanwhile holes will move from the

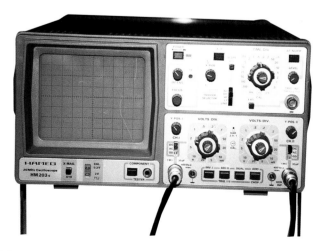

Many oscilloscopes employ transistors in circuits to amplify and display electrical signals.

1.

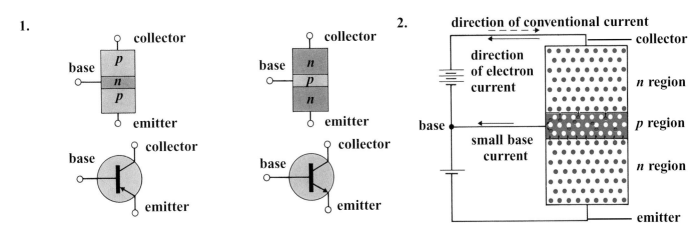

2.

These illustrations show how transistors are formed and how they work, (1) how simple pnp and npn type transistors are connected, (2) an npn bipolar transistor powered to act as an amplifier, and (3) two different types of n-channel field-effect transistors.

3. **Depletion type**

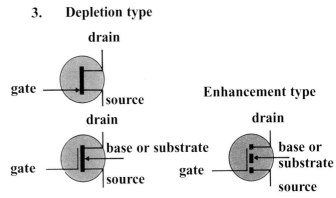

p-type side, across the junction, to the negative connection. When the battery connections are switched, electrons and holes pass straight to the connections without crossing the junction. Only the few stray electrons and holes of the original material will cross the junction, and these play an important part in the junction transistor.

JUNCTION TRANSISTORS

It is the sandwiching of a layer of *n* type between two layers of *p* type (*pnp* transistor), or a *p* type between two layers of *n* type (*npn* transistor) that creates a transistor. The center layer, which is always very thin, is known as the base. One side, which will be the negative connection, is known as the emitter. The other side, which will form the positive connection, is known as the collector.

> ### DID YOU KNOW?
>
> The transistor was invented in 1947 by American physicists John Bardeen (1908–1991), Walter Brattain (1902–1987), and William Shockley (1910–1989), who were working at the Bell Telephone Laboratories. In 1956 they were jointly awarded the Noble Prize in Physics for their work.

By layering the crystal into a sandwich, little current will flow through in either direction because the joining faces will block the action. When a small current is passed into the middle layer, the free electrons allow a current from the battery to pass through the sandwich.

What happens is that both electrons from the *n* type and holes from the *p* type carry the current, which has given the junction transistor its other name—bipolar transistor.

Electrons in an *npn* type transistor are far more numerous than holes because the *n*-type layer is given a greater dose of impurity than the base layer. The current passes through the base-emitter junction carried by the electrons from the emitter region and by the free electrons that are able to pass into the base from the emitter layer. These free electrons are also able to pass into the collector layer, thus enabling a magnified current to pass right through the sandwich.

Junction transistors need only a tiny amount of power to make them work—about one-thousandth of an amp. Yet when the current leaves the collector,

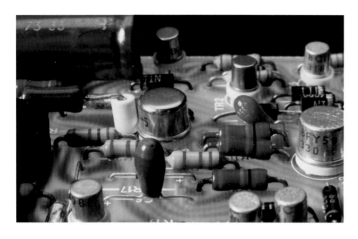

▲ *This smoke-detector circuit board contains a number of transistors (the silver components). Transistors can also be made much smaller. Microchips, for example, may contain many millions of tiny transistors.*

which can be thought of as an output terminal, it can be increased up to one hundred times. Thus the junction transistor is a high-gain current amplifier.

The difference between the *npn*-type transistor and a *pnp*-type transistor is in the direction of the flow of electrical current. In the *pnp* type, the collector will be connected to a negative supply terminal. In the *npn* type, the collector will be connected to a positive terminal.

FIELD EFFECT TRANSISTORS

Similar to the bipolar junction transistor, the field effect transistor (FET) has three terminals. They are called source (equal to the collector), gate (base), and drain (emitter). These transistors are divided into two types: the junction-gate FET (or JFET) and the insulated-gate FET (or IGFET).

Junction-gate FET

The junction-gate field effect transistor works in quite a different way from the junction transistor. Current in the JFET does not pass through the *pn* junction but flows through the *n*-type layer in a path called the channel. This is because the sandwich is arranged not as three flat layers, but one flat *p* layer and one thick *n* layer, with a small thick *p* layer set into its top center. The two *p* layers are connected and form the gate. On one side, the U-shaped *n* layer forms the source; on the other

side, it forms the drain. Current flowing through the channel between the two gate layers is controlled by the voltage into the gate (the *p*-type layers).

When no voltage is applied to the gate, the electrons in the *n* layer remain evenly scattered throughout the layer and can carry a current between source and drain. When a negative voltage is placed across the gate, the electrons in the *p* layer between source and drain are forced back from the gate because like charges repel each other.

There is now only a small channel of electrons between source and drain. The blank areas are called depletion areas. If the negative charge in the gate is increased, the electrons are forced to the far ends of the *n* layer. The depletion areas meet between the two gate layers and stop any current from passing between source and drain.

Insulated-gate FET

The insulated-gate field effect transistor (IGFET) is made up as a thick *p* layer (called the base or substrate), with two *n*-layer areas set in it. The two *n* layers, which are separate, are the source and drain. The gate is a layer of metal shielded (insulated) from the *p* layer by a thin strip of silicon dioxide (SiO_2). Because there is no connection between source and drain, no current can flow. When a positive voltage is put on the gate, free electrons are attracted from the two *n*-layer areas and the *p* layer. They rise toward the gate and form a layer of electrons between the two *n* layers—the source and drain. There is now a channel of electrons through which a current can flow. This is called an enhancement type IGFET.

It is also possible to make the IGFET with a built-in *n* channel. In this case, a negative voltage at the gate would cut the channel by repelling the electrons, so no current will flow. This is called a depletion type IGFET. IGFETs can also be made with two independent gates, which are used as frequency amplifiers and mixers in radio receivers.

> *See also:* ELECTRONICS • ELECTRON TUBE • MICROELECTRONICS • SEMICONDUCTOR • SILICON

Transition element

The transition elements are a group of metals with similar physical and chemical properties. These elements form three series (rows), called the transition series, in the middle of the periodic table of chemical elements. Important transition elements include chromium, copper, iron, gold, silver, titanium, tungsten, and the platinum group metals.

Russian chemist Dmitry Mendeleyev (1834–1907) constructed the first periodic table of chemical elements and was the first person to use the term *transition element*. Mendeleyev grouped together nine elements that had similar physical and chemical properties: iron, cobalt, nickel, ruthenium, rhodium, palladium, osmium, iridium, and platinum. The last six, apart from being transition elements, are also called the platinum group metals. Now the term *transition element* is used to describe the elements from scandium to zinc in the fourth period (a horizontal row of the periodic table), yttrium to cadmium in the fifth period, and hafnium to mercury in the sixth period.

Electron structure

Everything in the universe consists of tiny particles called atoms. Atoms are the building blocks of matter, but they are far too small to be seen with the

▼ *Gold is a highly prized precious metal in the third transition series. It is one of the least chemically reactive of the transition elements and can be found in nature as the pure metal.*

orbitals, called s, p, d, and f, and they have different shapes, which determine how many electrons they can hold. The s orbital can hold up to two electrons, the p orbital can hold up to six electrons, the d orbital can hold up to ten electrons, and the f orbital can hold up to 14 electrons.

The transition elements are often defined as those that have a partially filled d or f orbital. For example, scandium has an atomic number of 21, which means there are 21 electrons orbiting the nucleus of every scandium atom. The electrons fill up the atom in the following way. There are two electrons in the first electron shell, which comprises just one full s orbital. Eight electrons occupy the second electron shell, which comprises one full s orbital and one full p orbital. Nine electrons occupy the third electron shell, which comprises one s orbital, one p orbital, and one d orbital. The s and p orbitals are full, but the d orbital contains just one electron. The fourth electron shell contains two electrons in one full s orbital. Successive elements in the first transition series (from titanium through zinc) have more electrons in the d orbital, up to the maximum of ten, which corresponds to zinc. This pattern is repeated with elements from the second and third transition series.

Physical properties

The transition elements are ductile (can be drawn into a wire) and malleable (can be easily beaten into a sheet) metals. They also have high melting and boiling points. For example, titanium melts at 3034°F (1668°C) and boils at 5949°F (3287°C) and tungsten melts at 6192°F (3422°C) and boils at 10,031°F (5555°C). Transition elements are very dense—much denser than the alkali metals and the alkaline earth metals. Only a few other metals, such as tin and lead, have comparable densities.

The transition elements have a luster when clean and are good conductors of heat and electricity. The internal structure of some of the transition

naked eye—the period at the end of this sentence would cover around 250 billion atoms. Atoms are made up of even smaller particles, called electrons, neutrons, and protons. The neutrons and protons cluster together in the dense center, or nucleus, of the atom. The electrons revolve around the nucleus in orbits called electron shells, which correspond to the energy of the electrons within them.

Only a certain number of electrons can occupy each electron shell. For example, up to two electrons can occupy the electron shell nearest the nucleus, up to eight electrons can occupy the next electron shell, and up to 18 electrons can occupy the third electron shell. Electrons also travel in paths, called orbitals, within these electron shells. There are four different elements means that they can become brittle at low temperatures. Adding small amounts of impurities of other elements can make them much harder. For example, iron is comparatively soft when pure, but it is changed into the harder alloy steel when just 0.03 percent carbon is added.

Chemical properties

The chemical reactivity of the transition elements varies, ranging from fairly reactive metals, such as copper and iron, to extremely unreactive metals, such as silver and gold. However, all the transition elements form compounds such as salts, for example, chlorides and sulfates. Often, they do not have a characteristic valency, so they combine with other elements in different ways. For example, iron can form two chlorides: iron (II) chloride ($FeCl_2$) and iron (III) chloride ($FeCl_3$). Iron (II) chloride is also called ferric chloride, and iron (III) chloride is also called ferrous chloride.

One interesting property of the transition elements is the way in which they form complex ions. Transition element ions accept pairs of

> ### DID YOU KNOW?
>
> Swiss chemist Alfred Werner (1866–1919) won the 1913 Nobel Prize for chemistry for his work on the complex ions of the transition elements. Werner's theory, called coordination theory, allowed for a simple classification of inorganic compounds and added to the concept of isomerism, which is the relationship between chemicals that contain the same number of atoms of the same elements but differ in structural arrangement. Werner's coordination theory has been revised slightly, but it is still fundamental to modern inorganic chemistry, paving the way for modern concepts of chemical bonding.

▼ *Nickel is a silver-gray metal that resists attack by water and oxygen in the air under normal conditions. It is never found as a pure metal in Earth's crust; it is always found mixed with other elements, such as sulfur, in the form of compounds.*

▲ *Small amounts of chromium give this emerald its attractive green color.*

electrons from chemical groups called ligands, forming a covalent bond and resulting in the creation of the complex ion. In a water solution of copper sulfate ($CuSO_4$), for example, the copper forms complex ions with four water molecules (the ligands). Each ligand donates a pair of electrons to form a covalent bond with the copper ion, resulting in the complex ion $Cu(H_2O)_4^{2+}$. If ammonium hydroxide (NH_4OH) is added to the solution, ammonia (NH_3) acts as a ligand, replacing the water in the ion to form $Cu(NH_3)_4^{2+}$.

Many other ligands form complex ions with the transition elements. Metal carbonyl complexes are compounds, such as iron carbonyl ($Fe_2(CO)_9$), that contain carbon monoxide (CO) as the ligand. An extra pair of electrons on the carbon atom in carbon monoxide forms the bonds to the metal atoms in carbonyl compounds.

Color

Compounds of transition elements and their complex ions are noted for their bright colors. The different colors of gemstones are often due to impurities of transition elements. For example, chromium is responsible for the red of ruby as well as the green of emerald. Complex ions containing cobalt may range from red to blue.

Magnetic properties

The transition elements tend to be paramagnetic, which is weaker than the type of magnetism—called ferromagnetism—shown by iron, cobalt, and nickel. Complex mixtures of these three metals with additions of aluminum and titanium form the alnico group of magnetic alloys.

See also: ELEMENT, CHEMICAL • INORGANIC CHEMISTRY • PLATINUM GROUP METALS • SALT, CHEMICAL • TITANIUM • VALENCE

Truck

From coast to coast, across continents, a wide variety of trucks drive along highways carrying goods and raw materials between towns and cities. These huge vehicles are among the most up-to-date available, and research is constantly under way to improve their performance, economy, comfort, and safety.

It may not seem apparent, but under their familiar metal bodies, trucks continue to change a great deal. Much research and design work has been done to improve the efficiency of the engines, chassis, trailers, and cabs of these vehicles.

There are many reasons for these continuing developments. One of them is environmental, with great public and governmental pressure to make all forms of transportation as harmless to the world as possible in terms of noise and pollution. Another pressure is economic. Truck owners want to save fuel and become faster and more efficient to compete with other freight transportation systems, such as airlines and railroads. Another cause for concern is safety, for the truck driver and for other drivers on the highway.

Less stress for more safety

Psychologists (scientists who study people and their behavior) think that providing a good, comfortable working environment reduces the chance that a driver will become tired and stressed. The more alert and the less stressed a driver, the less likelihood that he or she will make an error that could lead to an accident.

For example, the color scheme within many truck cabs is carefully chosen to create a harmonious atmosphere. Soft, blending shades are used rather than garish, clashing colors that could lead to eye strain. Blues and greens, rather than hot reds, are

▲ *Trucks, such as this U.S. "rig" (truck and trailer), are a constant sight on highways all over the world. Trucks are a vital link in the supply chain that keeps business and industry supplied with goods and raw materials.*

favored for soothing overtones. The combination of tones and colors is used for everything from seat upholstery and trimming to carpeting.

Some long-distance truck cabins have sleeping bunks, and they may be as well equipped as a small apartment—with a refrigerator, stove, stereo, and hot and cold water.

The driver's seat is designed not only for comfort on a long journey, but also to cut down the amount of road vibration, which can badly affect the driver over long periods. Damping springs and rubber mounts are used for the suspended seats.

The position of the driver's seat is carefully calculated by a computer, as are the relative positions between the gear level, pedals, and steering wheel.

This is all done for the maximum efficiency and minimum strain on the driver. For this reason, too, the other controls, such as those for lights and wipers, are grouped within easy reach of the driver, who also has the clearest possible view of the instrument panel. The science behind the positioning and feel of controls is called ergonomics.

Cutting down noise and mechanical vibration

Because the truck acts as a sounding board, noise created in one area may be heard in another. Research has shown that the point of attachment

▼ *This picture shows the compressed-air braking system and transmission of a truck. The two pairs of wheels at the back of the truck give it good traction.*

between the driveline (the truck's power system) and the chassis must be chosen carefully for the least possible amount of noise and vibration.

Reduction of noise inside the cab is important for the health, safety, and comfort of the driver. Careful sound insulation means that the noise level can be made as low as that in many passenger cars.

This insulation also acts as a thermal barrier, keeping the cab cool in hot weather and warm in cold weather. Well-insulated cabs can maintain a temperature of 75°F (24°C) even when outside temperatures are as low as 14°F (−10°C). Because truck drivers spend a lot of time in their cabs, it is extremely important that they can drive in a comfortable atmosphere.

◀ *In many trucks the driver's cab is above the engine. This gives the driver a commanding view of the road and also makes the truck as short as possible. Most general maintenance of the engine can be done from under a hood at the front of the truck. To fully access the engine, however, the whole cab hinges forward.*

Computers in trucks

Trucks are equipped with a range of electronic instruments to assist the driver. Sensors may display or sound warnings in the cab to reveal problems such as under-inflated tires, wheel imbalance, wear on brakes, engine problems, and insecure loads.

In modern trucks, as in modern automobiles, computers are used widely. Central processing units (CPUs) are connected to the engine. CPUs measure the amount of oxygen entering the engine and then precisely adjust the amount of fuel supplied through electronic fuel injectors. This increases the efficiency of the engine. If the CPU detects that the engine speed is uneconomical for the gear ratio selected, a warning may sound.

Other computer systems used in trucks include navigation systems. Using Global Positioning System (GPS) satellites and preprogrammed maps, computerized navigation systems calculate the shortest or fastest route to a destination. They can also calculate the best average speed at which to drive to reach the destination on time and with the greatest fuel economy.

Turbocharged engines

Turbocharged engines are used on many trucks to improve their performance. A turbocharger is a turbine powered by the engine's exhaust gases. This turbine is connected by a shaft to a compressor, which forces air into the engine. By supplying air to the engine under pressure, more air, and therefore more oxygen, enters the engine. The more oxygen that enters an engine, the more fuel can be burned, and the more power the engine will produce. Turbochargers can increase the power output of an engine by up to 50 percent.

DID YOU KNOW?

The biggest trucks in the world are the "road trains" of Australia. These giant trucks have three or more trailers, are over 174 feet (53 meters) long, and weigh more than 150 tons (136 tonnes). Road trains are used to transport goods and livestock across Australia's vast outback.

▲ *Many trucks are designed for specialized uses. The truck in this photograph has a hydraulic mechanism used for collecting household garbage bins.*

The intercooler is used alongside the turbo-charger. As the air in the turbocharger is compressed, it heats and expands, resisting further compression. By cooling the air first, more of it can be forced into the inlet manifold. The result is a higher engine power output and improved economy. The benefits of turbocharging are particularly useful to trucks because they have to haul heavy loads and cover long distances.

Exterior improvements

Designers have tried to reduce the damage that heavy vehicles cause in collisions with other vehicles. Bumpers have been placed lower, and a safety skirt has been added around the sides, so trucks cannot overrun passenger cars. An energy-absorbing barrier at the rear of a long vehicle, called an underrider, moves on hydraulic struts to absorb the shock of a collision.

In addition, visibility is improved by the use of heated rear-view mirrors, rear-view cameras with a screen inside the cab, and proximity sensors that warn the driver when an obstruction is nearby.

Another advance in truck design is the use of glass-reinforced plastic (GRP) bodywork. GRP is lightweight, clean, and cheaper than steel or aluminum, and it resists rusting. Truck design is tending toward cleaner lines and improved aerodynamic shape, resulting in less energy consumption and better-looking trucks.

See also: AUTOMOBILE • INTERNAL COMBUSTION ENGINE • TURBINE

Tsunami

Tsunamis are gigantic ocean waves that strike coasts with great force. They may cause loss of life and much damage to property. Most sea waves are caused by winds, but tsunamis are triggered by violent geologic events, such as earthquakes and volcanic explosions on the seabed.

Tsunamis are often called tidal waves, but they are not related to tides. The term *tsunami* is Japanese for "harbor" (*tsu*) "wave" (*nami*). Japan has suffered more from these killer waves than any other country, although many other parts of the world can be affected by tsunamis.

What causes tsunamis?

Throwing a pebble into a pond disturbs the water and causes a series of ever-widening ripples to spread across the surface. Tsunamis are similar ripples but on a much larger scale. Tsunamis can be caused by any of three events—either an underwater earthquake (movement of the seafloor), a volcanic eruption into the sea, or a huge landslide.

Earthquakes happen when Earth's rocky crust slips along faults (cracks). During reverse faulting, the rocks on the ocean floor slump downward along a fault line so that a large depression is

▼ *This aerial photograph shows the devastation caused to Banda Aceh, Indonesia, after the massive tsunami struck on December 26, 2004. The tsunami struck coastlines across the region, killing an estimated 225,000 people.*

formed. Seawater rushes into this depression, causing a fast withdrawal of the sea from nearby coasts. This is often the only warning people have of a tsunami because the withdrawal of the water is soon followed by a surge of water toward the land. Tsunamis are also caused when rocks move upward along fault lines (normal faulting) because such vertical shifts in the seabed also cause a massive displacement of seawater, making it move back and forth in waves. The highest earthquake-generated tsunami ever recorded was estimated to be 278 feet (85 meters) high. It appeared on April 24, 1771, off Ishigaki Island, Japan.

A second cause of tsunamis is volcanoes. Volcanoes can produce tsunamis in a number of ways. These include the rapid deposit of material into an ocean due to explosive eruptions of molten or solid rock, eruptions of hot fragments of rock and gases moving at high speeds, or landslides, as well as volcanic earthquakes and even powerful airwaves created by large volcanic explosions.

Waves produced by volcanic tsunamis can be as high as those produced by the largest earthquakes. The most devastating volcanic tsunami recorded was the eruption in Krakatoa, Indonesia, in 1883. The waves reached heights of more than 130 feet (40 meters), killing 36,000 people.

Tsunamis are sometimes caused by coastal or underwater landslides, which are often the result of earthquakes but may also be caused by other geologic activity. One enormous landslide occurred in 1958 at Lituya Bay in the Gulf of Alaska,

DID YOU KNOW?

The deadliest and possibly the most destructive tsunami in history occurred off the coast of Indonesia on December 26, 2004. A massive undersea earthquake with a magnitude of 9.0 on the Richter scale (one of the highest magnitudes recorded) struck off the coast of the island of Sumatra. During the next few hours, a series of powerful tsunamis triggered by the earthquake spread out across the Indian Ocean, devastating hundreds of miles of surrounding coastline, as well as coastlines as far away as East Africa. Some reports claimed that the waves had reached a height of 30 feet (9 meters) or more when they hit the shoreline. Although there is no official record, it is estimated that at least 225,000 people were killed across a dozen countries, with India, Indonesia, the Maldives, Sri Lanka, and Thailand, in particular, sustaining massive damage.

southeast of the Malaspina Glacier. This landslide produced the largest tsunami ever recorded. A huge wall of water moving at 130 miles (209 kilometers) per hour swept down the inlet. In some places, the surging water rose to 1,740 feet (530 meters). The massive body of water was so powerful that the landscape of the bay was completely reshaped.

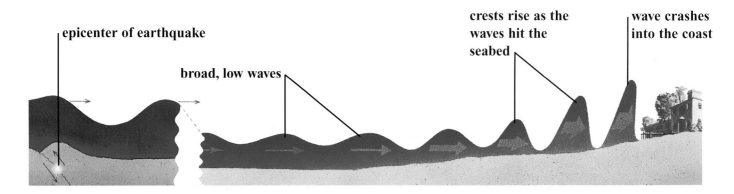

epicenter of earthquake

broad, low waves

crests rise as the waves hit the seabed

wave crashes into the coast

▲ *Many tsunamis are caused by large underwater earthquakes. These earthquakes displace huge volumes of water, causing a series of waves. As the waves reach shallow coastal waters, they speed up and become larger.*

▲ *A tsunami generated by an earthquake thousands of miles away in the Aleutian Islands, Alaska, washes over Laie Point on Oahu, Hawaii, on March 9, 1957. Much damage was done, but fortunately, no lives were lost.*

How tsunamis move

The successive waves of a tsunami travel quickly in deep water, often at speeds of hundreds of miles an hour. However, the wave lengths (the distances between successive crests) may be hundreds of miles apart, although the wave heights (the vertical distances between the crests and the troughs) are often no more than 2 to 3 feet (0.6 to 0.9 meter). Because the wave heights are so low, sailors on ships may not be aware of the passing of a tsunami. When the waves reach shallower waters near the shore, however, they are slowed down by friction with the rising sea bottom. As the velocity of the waves lessen, their wavelengths become shortened, and the amplitudes increase, creating large and destructive waves. The succeeding outflow of water is often just as destructive as the incoming waves.

Where tsunamis occur

More than 500 tsunamis have been recorded in the last 2,500 years, and most of them have occurred in the Pacific Ocean. The Pacific is bordered by the "ring of fire," a zone where earthquakes and volcanoes are common. Evidence suggests that only the most intense earthquakes create tsunamis.

In cooperation with other nations and agencies, the U.S. National Weather Service set up a Tsunami Warning System that provides information about large waves to 14 Pacific coastal and inland nations. However, tsunamis may occur elsewhere, such as in the Indian Ocean. One of the reasons for the huge loss of life in the 2004 Indonesian tsunami was lack of an early warning system. Since the disaster, discussions have taken place to implement a regional tsunami warning system in that part of the world.

See also: EARTHQUAKE • OCEAN • PLATE TECTONICS • VOLCANO • WAVE MOTION

Tunneling

Tunnels are enclosed passages under the ground or a body of water. They are also dug through high mountains. Tunnels are built for subway trains in crowded cities and for trains and cars to travel between places separated by rivers or mountains. Early tunnels were dug by hand, but tunneling machines now make the job much easier.

A tunnel is any passageway below a surface—even an underpass connecting two sides of a street. However, the great challenges to tunnel builders have been the long stretches of road under land or water or through mountains that are part of so many of the world's road and railroad systems.

Early tunnels were built through hard rock so that a natural roof was formed. These tunnels were sometimes impressive engineering feats. In Naples, Roman engineers built a road tunnel 3,000 feet (914 meters) long. With the coming of the canals and railroads in the nineteenth century, longer tunnels were needed, often through soft or wet ground. Consequently, new construction methods had to be developed.

Tunnel shields

The most important advance in tunnel engineering was the invention of the tunnel shield in 1818 by British inventor and engineer Marc Isambard Brunel (1769–1849). The tunnel shield was used for two early tunnels built under the River Thames in London, England. The design was improved by British engineer James Henry Greathead (1844–1896) and used when constructing the London subway system.

▶ *Huge tunnel boring machines such as the one in this picture were used during the construction of the Channel Tunnel between Britain and France, which opened in 1994.*

The modern shield is a movable frame in the shape of a cylinder that supports the surface of the tunnel as it is being dug. This allows the workers to remove dirt and rocks as they are loosened and to install the permanent lining of the tunnel.

The shield is made of steel with a sharp edge. As the shield is driven ahead, the cutting edge shapes the tunnel. Powerful hydraulic jacks are mounted at the back of the shield, and these push the shield forward as the tunnel progresses.

Hard ground tunneling

For tunneling through hard ground without a machine, the rock face is drilled with holes that will carry explosives. These holes are drilled slightly

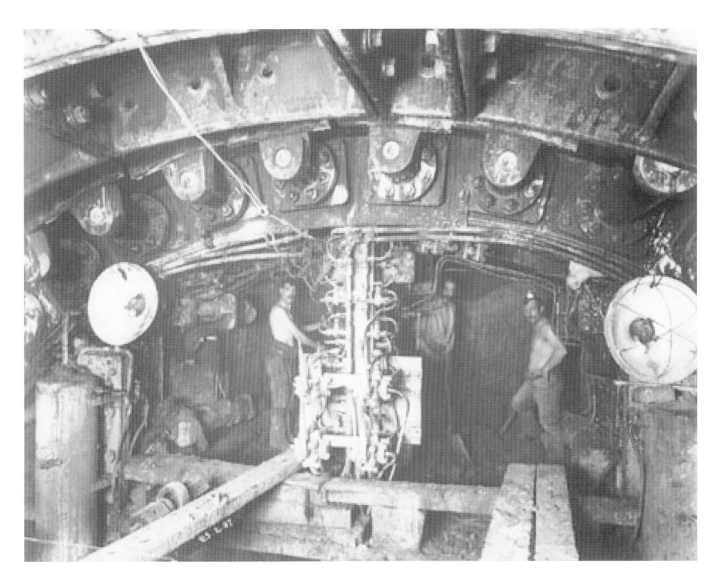

▲ *This picture shows two sections of tunneling shield in use during the excavation of the Rotherhithe road tunnel in London, England, in 1907. As the shield is driven into the ground by hydraulic rams, the miners excavate the earth from the middle of the tunnel.*

inward so that the rock is blown back into the center of the tunnel. The explosives are arranged in a careful pattern so that each explosion will break up a large depth of rock. Explosives are put into the holes and are set to go off at different times to better control the way in which the rock fragments, and thus the shape of the tunnel.

Soft-ground tunneling

Mining methods were first used to tunnel through soft ground. Horizontal boards were placed close together and were supported by vertical boards to make a roof. Where the digging took place, the surface had to be closely boarded. These boards were removed one at a time so that a small area of ground could be dug out. The board would then be placed a short distance ahead. Progress was slow, as great care had to be taken to hold back the earth at the sides and top of the tunnel.

Excavating machines

Modern tunnels are dug by specially designed excavating machines. With a full-face machine, the entire front face of the shield turns. For hard ground and rock, the edges of the tunnel are cut by sharp teeth on rollers or disks.

Partial-face machines are mounted on rails and have a single cutting head attached to an arm. This arm can be moved over the entire area of the tunnel face by hydraulic controls. Sometimes the arm is mounted within a tunnel shield, with the shape of the cutting controlled by a guide ring.

A method was also developed for tunneling by machine through sand and gravel containing water. Bentonite, a clay type of mineral, is applied under pressure to the tunnel surface to stabilize the soft ground during digging. The excavated material is mixed with the bentonite and water and pumped to the surface. The bentonite is separated from the sand or gravel and can be used again at the tunnel surface.

Tunnel linings

The material chosen to line the inside of a tunnel must be able to stand up to a number of forces. For instance, the tunnel shield pushes against the lining

▼ *This is the rear of a tunneling machine used in the Channel Tunnel. Behind the cutting face, boring machines have systems of conveyor belts to transport debris away and hydraulic rams to push tunnel liners against the walls of the tunnel.*

DID YOU KNOW?

The longest road tunnel in the world is the Laerdal tunnel in Norway, which is 15 miles (24.5 kilometers) long and runs under a mountain between Aurland and Laerdal. Drilling started in 1995, and the breakthrough occurred four years later. During construction, there was a large fall of rock from the roof, caused by the weak nature of the rock and immense pressure from the mountain above. Engineers filled the site of the rockfall with concrete and then proceeded to drill through the concrete and rubble. Great care was taken in the design of the tunnel to improve safety. Feelings of claustrophobia are reduced by the tunnel's long curves and occasional openings into spacious caverns.

▲ *This is the west entrance to the Cheung Ching Tunnel in Hong Kong. Once a tunnel has been dug and lined, utilities such as electricity and water have to be installed, as well as paving or rail tracks and signs.*

during construction, and then it must be able to hold the loads from above. The first linings were made of wood or brick. Cast-iron rings were introduced at the end of the nineteenth century. Cast iron is expensive today, and precast concrete segments are often used instead. If a lining is needed in hard rock tunnels, concrete is used.

Underwater tunnels

A two-hundred-year-old dream became a reality when the Channel Tunnel, linking Britain and France, opened in 1994. The tunnel runs under the English Channel, from Dover, England, to Calais, France. Of the tunnel's total of 31 miles (50 kilometers), 23½ miles (37.5 kilometers) are underwater. The tunnel runs through a clay-containing limestone called chalk marl. It is an almost completely watertight material and easy to dig through. The Channel Tunnel has two tunnels for high-speed electric trains, plus a smaller service

tunnel between them. Six machines were used to dig the tunnel, while workers at the rear attached concrete panels to the tunnel walls as lining.

Considered one of the great engineering accomplishments of the twentieth century, the Seikan Tunnel in Japan opened in 1988 after 24 problem-filled years of work. The Seikan Tunnel connects the islands of Honshu and Hokkaido. It is 33½ miles (53.8 kilometers) in length and it, too, is a railroad tunnel—the longest in the world. Because they ran into weak and cracked rock while digging the tunnel, engineers changed from tunnel-boring machines to drill-and-blast methods to continue boring the tunnel. They solved a severe flooding problem by injecting a type of grout with great force into holes drilled in the tunnel walls. The grout would seep into cracks and become solid, keeping water out. The walls were lined with shotcrete, a form of concrete that is sprayed on, filling cracks and making the tunnel stronger.

See also: DRILL • EXPLOSIVE • HYDRAULICS • MINING AND QUARRYING

Turbine

The word *turbine* means "something that spins." When people talk about turbines, they usually mean wheels driven by moving water, steam, or gas. These wheels are used to work ship and airplane engines and the generators that make electricity.

The idea of using moving water or air to drive machinery is centuries old. Since earliest times, people have used waterwheels and windmills to grind corn. Windmills are still widely used in many parts of the world to operate water pumps.

Both windmills and water wheels consist mainly of a large wheel with sails or paddles that are moved—in one case by the wind and in the other by moving water.

A waterwheel, for example, operates when falling water strikes the paddles or buckets around its edge and forces the wheel to rotate. Because only a fraction of the water falling on the wheel actually strikes a paddle, much of it is wasted.

In the nineteenth century, scientists realized that such waste could be avoided if the wheel could be enclosed, and all the water needed to turn it channeled through the chamber. In effect, this is what people know today as a turbine.

Modern turbines operate with water, gas, or steam. In all cases, the energy of the moving material—water, gas, or steam—is converted by the turbine into a form of energy people can use. This may be to drive a ship or an airplane, or it may be converted by a generator into electricity, for which we have thousands of uses.

Water turbines

One of the first examples of a water turbine was a small motor built in England by Robert Barker around 1743. This rotary (revolving) engine got its power from water jets coming out of a sprinkler,

▲ *Wind farms such as this one near Tarifa, Spain, have been built in many remote, windy areas. These turbines use the power of the wind to generate electricity. Power produced in this way does not damage the environment.*

which acted on another wheel to create movement. It seemed more like a toy than a working machine, but Barker's idea was developed later.

In 1743, a French scientist working in England built a turbine along the same lines as Barker's motor, but it was not very powerful. More than 30 years passed before another French scientist improved on the earlier turbine, but even his version was never put into use. Finally, in 1839, Scottish engineer James Whitelaw built one that actually was used. It produced up to 100 horsepower.

The next improvement in water turbines came from French engineer Benoit Fourneyron (1802–1867) and his teacher Claude Burdin. Having experimented with the idea of a rotary engine for years, they built a successful working turbine for which they won a prize. It was a reaction turbine in which water flowed out of the bottom of a tank through vanes that guided the flow into a set of moving blades. These were connected to and moved the working wheel. Burdin made up the word *turbine* from the Latin for "spinning top."

Another kind of turbine is called the impulse engine. Its rotation is caused by a high-speed jet of water hitting the blades of a wheel to rotate it.

In the late nineteenth century, more work was done on impulse turbines. The most widely known were built with buckets around the outer edge of a wheel. The wheel would be moved by a high-speed jet of water directed into the buckets.

Hydroelectric power

Electricity made by a turbine that is operated by flowing or falling water is called hydroelectric power (HEP). The blades of the turbine are mounted in a shaft. As the water strikes the turbine blades, they revolve. This spins the shaft of the turbine, which is connected to a generator.

The turbines need a constant flow of water to work efficiently. There are two aspects of the water flow that are important—the volume and the head of the water. The head is the distance the water must fall before it strikes the turbine rotor (wheel). A head can be as little as 8 feet (2.4 meters) or, when water from a mountain is used to turn turbines in a valley below, it may be as much as 1,000 feet (300 meters).

The design of the turbine depends on the size of the head and the volume of water. There are two kinds of turbines, impulse and reactor.

In an impulse turbine, the rotor can be mounted on a horizontal or a vertical shaft. The ends of the turbine blades act as cup-shaped buckets, into which jets of water are directed at high speed, forcing the blades to turn. Impulse turbines are best suited to places where the head of water is high.

The reactor turbines works best at low-head sites where there is a large volume of water. The turbine is underwater and is turned by the weight of the water as well as the speed at which it is flowing.

The turbine is on a vertical shaft and usually has one of two types of blades. These can be Francis-type blades or Kaplan-type blades (both named for their inventors.) Francis-type blades are spirally curved and are suitable for low- and high-

◄ *These are steam turbines in a nuclear power plant. Steam turbines are among the most powerful machines in use and, like water-powered turbines, they are used to generate electricity. A million-kilowatt turbine generator can supply all the electricity used by a million people. The power of steam turbines is also used to propel ships and work pumps.*

head sites. The Francis-type turbine is still the most commonly used type. Kaplan-type blades are best suited to low-head sites. This type of blade looks something like a ship's propeller. The pitch (slant) of the blades can be adjusted to allow different amounts of water to flow through the turbine. Reactor turbines also have gates and valves that help to control the flow of water over the blades.

Steam turbines

In principle, a steam turbine works in much the same way as a water-driven turbine. A jet of extremely hot steam is forced through an enclosed space. As the steam rushes through the turbine tube, it turns the rotor blades of the turbine. In turn, these spin the shaft on which they are held. The shaft then turns the generator, or whatever machine is being operated by the turbine. Large

steam turbines are often designed with both reactor and impulse blades, carried by several rotors in separate casings.

Steam enters the turbine at an extremely high temperature, as much as 1050°F (565°C), which is five times the temperature of boiling water. As well as being hot, the steam is under great pressure, at about 2,000 pounds per square inch (140 kilograms per square centimeter). It rushes through the turbine at 1,000 miles (1,600 kilometers) per hour.

▼ *This diagram shows a single-stage steam turbine. The steam, controlled by the inlet valve governing mechanism, enters the turbine through the inlet valve. As it passes through the nozzle passages, the steam loses pressure and expands as a result. This forces the steam through the blades, turning them rapidly. The steam then passes out of the turbine through the steam outlet to the condenser, where it is cooled.*

1 inlet valve governing mechanism
2 inlet valve
3 steam nozzle
4 speed reduction gears
5 moving blades (first set)
6 moving blades (second set)
7 fixed blades
8 steam outlet

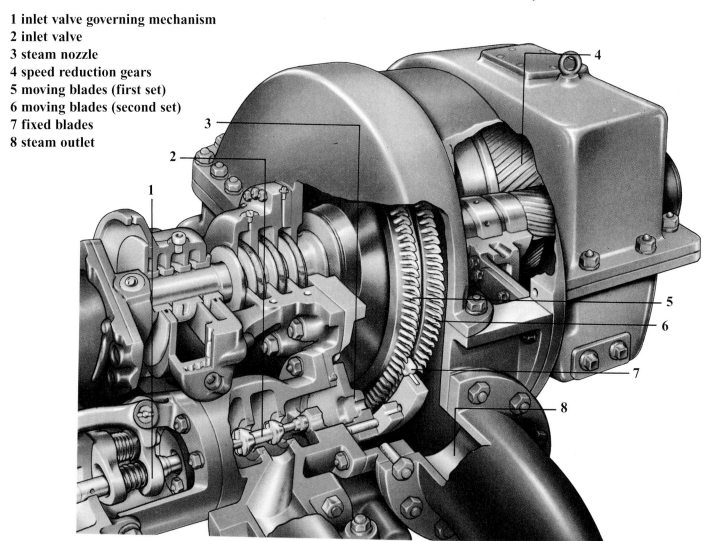

▶ *Engineers assemble a gas turbine. Gas turbines operate at higher temperatures than steam turbines. They must therefore be made from metals that will keep their strength and shape at temperatures of 2000°F (1093°C) or more. The hotter the turbine, the more efficiently it runs.*

A steam turbine contains several—sometimes as many as 24—wheels on a horizontal shaft. In front of each rotor there is a fixed ring holding blade-shaped nozzles. The steam passes over each rotor and then passes through the nozzles, which direct it onto the next rotor, and so on. Modern steam turbines have rotors of both the impulse and reactor types at various stages along the shaft. The steam expands in volume as it passes through the turbine, so the rotors and nozzles must be made larger the farther along the shaft they fall.

At the far end of the turbine shaft, there is a condenser, which cools the steam and turns it into water. Water takes up only a tiny fraction of the space of low-pressure steam, so when cooled, it creates a vacuum. This vacuum pulls steam into it, thus forcing it through the turbine.

In a fraction of a second, the steam passing through the condenser drops in temperature from 1050°F (565°C) to 100°F (38°C). The pressure inside the condenser drops from 2,000 pounds per square inch (140 kilograms per square centimeter) to ½ pound per square inch (0.04 kilograms per square centimeter).

To heat the water to create steam, another source of energy is needed. This is usually a fuel such as coal, gas, or oil, which is burned. In a nuclear power station, the water is turned to steam by the heat created when a nuclear reactor splits atoms in a process called fission.

Steam turbines work at high temperatures for days or even months without stopping. They must therefore be made of especially strong steel that can withstand this amount of work.

Gas turbines

Gas turbines, as their name suggests, work using gas instead of steam or water. To run a gas turbine, air is drawn into the turbine and compressed. It is then forced into a combustion chamber, where it is mixed with vaporized fuel and burned. The gases created when this happens expand and rush through the back of the turbine, spinning sets of turbine rotors as they do.

Some of the power created in this way is used to drive the compressor. The rest powers pumps, generators, ships, or other devices. In a jet airplane, the burning gases that are not used to power the compressor are forced out the back of the engine as a powerful jet to provide thrust.

See also: GAS TURBINE • HYDROELECTRIC POWER • JET ENGINE

Ultrasonics

Not all sound can be heard by people. The vibrations that cause some sounds are too fast for the human ear to follow, so those sounds are outside the range of human hearing. The name for the study of sounds of this type is ultrasonics. Ultrasonics has important uses in both industry and medicine.

Sound travels in waves produced by rapid vibrations in a medium. The medium may be air or water, or any other substance in which vibrations can occur. A medium consists of tiny particles, called atoms and molecules, and these particles move rapidly back and forth when they are disturbed.

As the sound wave travels through the medium, the vibrations cause temporary pressure differences within the medium by compressing some of the particles and spreading others out. For this reason, sound waves are known as compressional waves.

The number of vibrations that occur in one second is called the frequency of the wave. Frequency is measured in units called hertz (Hz), named for German physicist Heinrich Hertz (1857–1894). Waves also have a wavelength and an amplitude. The wavelength is simply the distance the sound travels in the time it takes a particle to complete one vibration. The amplitude is the distance the particle moves in one direction before moving back in the opposite direction.

Compressional waves that can be detected by the human ear have frequencies of between 20 and 20,000 hertz. They are called audible sounds because they are sounds that can be heard. Above 20,000 hertz, compressional waves are too fast for the human ear to detect, so they are not heard by human beings. However, these sound waves can be heard by some animals, such as dogs and bats. These sounds are said to be ultrasonic.

▼ *Ultrasonic sounds cannot be heard by people, but some animals, such as dogs and bats, can hear them. Bats can also produce ultrasonic sounds, which they use as a type of radar to navigate and find prey.*

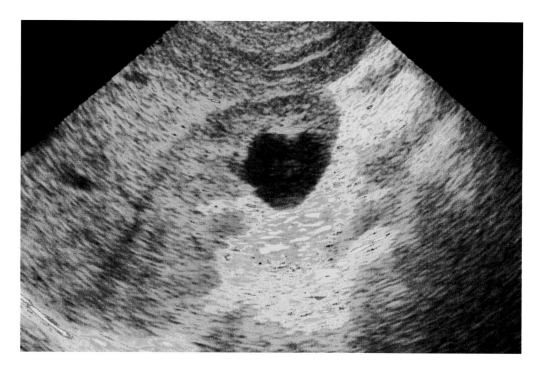

▶ *Ultrasound is used in medicine to produce images of the inside of people's bodies. This ultrasound picture shows a cyst that has formed on a patient's kidney.*

Using ultrasonic generators, it is possible to produce sound waves with frequencies of up to ten billion hertz. In theory, however, the frequency of an ultrasonic wave is unlimited.

Producing ultrasonic waves

Ultrasonic waves, which are high-frequency sound vibrations, are produced in much the same way as audible sound, except that their source must be made to vibrate very quickly.

Most ultrasonic generators produce these fast vibrations by converting electrical or magnetic energy into mechanical energy. Such convertors are called transducers. Three types of transducer are commonly used in ultrasonic generation: piezoelectric, electrostrictive, and magnetostrictive.

Piezoelectric transducers

When a quartz crystal is subjected to pressure, it develops electrically charged surfaces. This is called the piezoelectric effect. The crystals that experience the effect—notably quartz and Rochelle salt—are called piezoelectric crystals. When sound waves strike a piezoelectric crystal, the variations in pressure produced cause an electrical current that varies according to the wave pattern. The crystal can thus be used to detect compressional waves.

This also works the other way around. Applying an alternating current (AC) to the crystal causes corresponding pressure changes that make the crystal vibrate. The greatest effect is produced when the crystal is made to vibrate at its natural mechanical frequency, a condition known as resonance. For this to happen, each crystal must be cut in a precise way.

The difficulty of cutting single piezoelectric crystals has been overcome by using ceramic materials, such as barium titanate ($BaTiO_3$). These materials contain piezoelectric areas and are able to act as transducers, although they must first be exposed to a strong electric field.

Magnetostrictive transducers

An AC passed through the coil of an electromagnet causes a magnetic rod at the center of the coil to keep changing its length. As the current moves in one direction, the rod becomes longer; as the current moves in the other direction, the rod becomes shorter again. This is called the magnetostriction effect, and it is due to the changing magnetic field set up by the AC. A magnetostrictive transducer works on this principle. The stretching and shrinking of the rod is a vibration that generates a compressional wave.

The process can also be reversed and used to detect ultrasonic waves. Ultrasonic vibrations will cause vibrations in the magnetic rod, causing changes in the magnetic field. The changes in the magnetic field can then be detected by changes in current in the surrounding coil.

Materials that are most suitable for the magnetostrictive effect include nickel, nickel alloys, and a group of metal oxides known as ferrites. Unlike piezoelectric crystals, these materials can be cut into any convenient shape.

Electrostrictive transducers

Just as a changing magnetic field can distort the shape of certain materials to produce high-frequency mechanical vibrations, so too can an electric field. This is known as the electrostrictive effect. As in the case of magnetostriction, the frequency of the mechanical vibrations produced by the electrostrictive effect is twice that of the applied field.

This effect is also reversible, so electrostrictive devices can be used as wave detectors or generators. The materials most commonly used for these

> **DID YOU KNOW?**
>
> Liquids that do not normally mix, such as oil and water, can be turned into a mixture called an emulsion under the influence of an ultrasonic beam. An ultrasonic beam can also force air bubbles out of molten metal before it is cast.

include the titanates of barium, calcium, and lead. These ceramic materials have several advantages over the piezoelectric crystals. They can, for example, be manufactured into different shapes as required, and they can produce rapid vibrations at much lower voltages.

Ultrasonics in industry

Ultrasonic waves cannot be produced as easily as sound waves within the audible range, but they are more convenient to use. To direct a narrow beam of audible sound waves, the generating source must be large compared with the vibration wavelength. Ultrasonic waves can have much

◀ *This technician is checking for damage to pipes at a chemical plant. Technicians often employ ultrasonic devices to test the integrity of various materials and structures.*

◀ *These scientists are developing an ultrasonic drilling machine for use in a space mission. The drill will allow samples of rocks to be taken. Ultrasonic drills do not rotate like conventional drills; rather they make ultrasonic vibrations to break up the materials being drilled.*

higher frequencies and therefore much shorter wavelengths than audible sound, so they need much smaller wave generators.

One important industrial use of ultrasonics is in the testing of different materials. It is replacing the more expensive (and more dangerous) radiographic methods. An ultrasonic pulse fed into a test piece of material through a transducer travels through the object until it meets a discontinuity— something that causes the pulse to be reflected. The discontinuity might be the opposite face of the object, some defect in the material, a hole, or simply something that should not be there. The position of the discontinuity can then be found from the speed and timing of the pulse.

Ultrasonic methods are also used in industry to aid the action of cleaning solvents. When an ultrasonic beam is generated in a fluid, it creates tiny gaps in the fluid. When ultrasonics are used with cleaning fluids, dirt particles from the machinery being cleaned are drawn into the gaps in the fluid.

A method of welding has been developed in which ultrasonic vibrations produce so much friction (rubbing together) between two surfaces touching each other that the heat generated is enough to weld them together.

Ultrasonics in medicine

The various types of tissues in the human body, such as bone, muscle, and fat, all reflect ultrasonic waves differently. A person can be scanned with an ultrasonic beam, and the different echoes produced can be recorded electronically and displayed on a screen to provide a picture, called an ultrasonograph. This method is used by obstetricians to follow the progress of a fetus in its mother's uterus, and for examining the brain for early signs of a tumor. An ultrasonograph is similar to an X-ray, except that the person is not exposed to the risks of harmful radiation.

Ultrasonics at sea

Ultrasonic beams are not as easily absorbed by water as are lower-frequency audible sound waves. They can, therefore, be used for depth sounding— measuring the depth of the water by bouncing the beams off the seabed—and for building up a map of underwater rock layers. This information is useful when looking for mineral deposits such as oil.

See also: ELECTROMAGNETISM • PIEZOELECTRICITY • RESONANCE • SOUND • WAVE MOTION

Ultraviolet

Light is energy in the form of waves. White light consists of a mixture of colors, and each color has a different wavelength. Red light has the longest waves, and violet light has the shortest waves. Ultraviolet is similar to other colors of light, but people cannot see it because the waves are shorter than the waves of white light.

The different colors of white light can be seen by looking at a rainbow or at light that has passed through a triangular block of glass called a prism. The shortest violet waves that people can see have wavelengths of 0.000016 inch (0.00041 millimeter). The waves of ultraviolet light range from this length down to about one hundred times shorter.

There are three groups of ultraviolet waves: the near ultraviolet (the longest), the middle ultraviolet, and the far ultraviolet (the shortest).

The Sun's energy

The Sun sends energy to Earth in the form of different kinds of waves, called electromagnetic radiation. One form of electromagnetic radiation is white light, but the Sun also emits ultraviolet waves, not all of which reach Earth. Far-ultraviolet waves cannot pass through Earth's atmosphere (the protective blanket of gases that surround the planet). This is just as well because far-ultraviolet waves are harmful to the body. However, some ultraviolet rays do pass through. Middle-ultraviolet

▼ *Long-wave ultraviolet lights, also called blacklights, are popular in nightclubs. When ultraviolet radiation strikes an object, the energy excites the atoms of the object, making it glow in an effect called fluorescence.*

waves are the ones that cause skin to tan or to become sunburned. Too much sunbathing causes skin cancer, especially on certain types of skin.

Fluorescence

People cannot see ultraviolet light, but directing near-ultraviolet waves onto certain substances (such as minerals, oils, and certain chemicals) makes them emit visible light, and they shine in the dark—an effect called fluorescence. This happens because the ultraviolet light gives more energy to the molecules of the substance. As the molecules return to their normal state, they give out fluorescent light. This property is useful for identifying minerals. It is also used in theaters and nightclubs for creating visual effects.

Fluorescent lamps

Fluorescence can be put to other uses as well. Ultraviolet lights, or blacklights, are made by passing electricity through a glass tube containing mercury vapor. The electrons in the mercury gain energy from the electrical current. They lose the energy as ultraviolet waves and fluorescent light. The inside of the glass tube is coated with different materials. This prevents the far-ultraviolet waves from escaping, leaving just the near-ultraviolet waves, which produce the fluorescent light. Different substances used as coatings can also produce different colors of light.

This type of ultraviolet lighting has many uses in industry, such as testing materials, identifying ores in mining, and lighting the instrument panels in the cockpits of airplanes. It is also useful in studying old documents.

> ### DID YOU KNOW?
>
> In dentistry, a type of ultraviolet light gun is used in the repair of chipped teeth. The instrument is about the size of a handheld hair dryer. The ultraviolet rays harden the resin that is used to rebuild the chipped parts of teeth.

▲ *Fish-farm water pours from a chamber containing an ultraviolet light. By irradiating the water with ultraviolet light, it is sterilized. Far-ultraviolet radiation is toxic so it will destroy any harmful waterborne microorganisms.*

Sun lamps

Sun lamps work in the same way as fluorescent lamps. However, they are coated with quartz or fluorite, which allows the middle-ultraviolet waves (the ones that tan the skin) to pass through. These waves are dangerous to the eyes, so anyone using a sun lamp must wear special glasses. Too much use of a sun lamp can be dangerous and might even cause skin cancer. Most sun lamps also have an infrared element that gives out heat.

Medical uses of ultraviolet

Ultraviolet light is helpful in the field of medicine. It is used in the treatment of skin diseases, such as acne, psoriasis, and lupus vulgaris (tuberculosis of the skin), as well as in the treatment of some other forms of tuberculosis. Ultraviolet radiation is also used to disinfect wounds, and research has shown that it can help to heal them.

Ultraviolet light helps the body make vitamin D, which is vital for the development of bones. People who have a disease called rickets, which is caused by a lack of vitamin D in the diet, may be treated with controlled exposure to ultraviolet radiation.

Other uses

Far-ultraviolet waves can kill harmful micro-organisms, so they are used to sterilize foods, water, and the air in operating theaters. As these waves are harmful to human skin, people working with or near them have to be very careful.

Ultraviolet is also used in space. A Geiger-Müller detector that is sensitive to ultraviolet waves can be mounted inside a rocket. As the rocket goes into

▲ A Mexican passport is held under ultraviolet light. This reveals the white symbol at right, which is printed using a fluorescent ink that is only visible in ultraviolet light. This security feature shows that the passport is genuine; its absence is used to detect forgeries.

space, the Geiger-Müller detector scans the skies for ultraviolet radiation, which would come from clouds of gases in the spaces between the stars.

Ultraviolet spectroscopy is a useful way of analyzing different substances based on their ability to absorb or emit ultraviolet light. Astronomers use this technique to learn more about the composition of celestial bodies, such as stars and galaxies.

Ultraviolet light can also be used to initiate some chemical reactions. For example, some adhesives can be cured (set) almost immediately using an ultraviolet lamp. These types of adhesives are particularly useful in dentistry. The fading of dyes that can occur in sunlight is another example of a chemical reaction initiated by ultraviolet light.

See also: DENTISTRY • LIGHT • SPECTROSCOPY

Universe

The universe is everything that exists, and it is larger than anyone could ever imagine. Astronomers have only just begun to learn how and when the universe was born, and they have even predicted how it might end.

Ideas about the universe have changed radically through the ages. To prehistoric peoples, the universe was simply part of the world where they happened to live, as well as the celestial bodies that could be seen in the sky above them. As the first great civilizations grew in the Middle East and Far East, however, people began to think more about what the universe was like.

For thousands of years, most people thought that Earth was flat. The ancient Hindu civilization in India thought that the flat Earth was carried on the backs of elephants and that the elephants stood on the backs of turtles that swam in a vast ocean.

The ancient Egyptian idea of the universe was that the flat Earth floated on the bottomless waters of the underworld. Spanning the heavens was the star-spangled body of the sky goddess Nut. The Sun was carried across the sky each day in a boat by the god Ra. Because ancient people could not explain the universe, they made up mystical tales about it that involved gods and supernatural happenings.

Ancient Greek philosophers decided that Earth must have the form of a sphere. They thought that the circle was the perfect shape and therefore most suitable for Earth, which they regarded as the center of the universe. These ideas were adopted by Greek astronomer Ptolemy (lived second century CE), who wrote them down in a book called *Almagest*.

▶ **This artist's impression shows the formation of the universe following the big bang. A huge release of energy shortly after the big bang triggered an event called inflation, blowing up the universe from smaller than an atom to bigger than a galaxy.**

In Ptolemy's universe, the Moon, the Sun, and the known planets revolved around a spherical Earth, which was stationary. The stars were fixed to the inside of a great dark celestial sphere, which also revolved around Earth. Some people thought that the sphere was dotted with holes, similar to a colander, and that the stars were the light beams that shone through from a celestial furnace outside.

The Copernican revolution

An Earth-centered view of the universe could not explain events such as the looping and occasional backward motion of the planets in the sky. Still, it was accepted, almost without question, until the sixteenth century. Then, in 1543, Polish astronomer Nicolaus Copernicus (1473–1543) suggested that the Sun was the center of the universe and that Earth was a mere planet revolving around the Sun along with the other planets.

Copernicus's theory upset the Catholic Church, who supported the idea that Earth was the center of the universe. As a result, anyone who agreed with Copernicus was branded a heretic. However, evidence in favor of Copernicus's theory began to

▶ *The National Radio Astronomy Observatory (NRAO) is home to a group of 27 radio telescopes that span 26 miles (40 kilometers) near Socorro, New Mexico. Astronomers use the telescopes to probe fundamental questions in astronomy and physics.*

accumulate. In particular, Italian scientist Galileo Galilei (1564–1642) made accurate observations of the sky using a telescope. Galileo came to support Copernicus's theory, but he was tried by the Inquistion and narrowly escaped execution.

Eventually, astronomers began to accept that the Sun was a star like any other star in the sky. Work by British astronomers William Herschel (1738–1822) and his son John Herschel (1792–1871), among others, suggested that all the stars in the sky belonged to a great "star island," or galaxy, in space. To them, this galaxy was the universe.

A great breakthrough in telescope technology came at the beginning of the twentieth century. In 1917, the 100-inch (254-centimeter) Hooker Telescope was constructed at the Mount Wilson Observatory in California. Astronomers such as the American Edwin Hubble (1889–1953) began to observe details in certain clouds, called nebulas, between the stars. Unlike ordinary nebulas, which consist of clouds of gases, astronomers saw that these nebulas were made up of even more stars. In fact, they were other galaxies.

In time, many more galaxies were identified. Hubble discovered that almost all of them were moving away from Earth, headlong through space. The farther away these galaxies, the faster they were moving. The universe therefore appeared to be expanding. The idea of an expanding universe is the cornerstone of modern study of the origin and development of the universe. This branch of space science is called cosmology.

The scale of the universe

No one knows the true size of the universe. It may have a definite size, or it may be infinitely enormous. For astronomers, however, there has always been a practical limit to the universe—the part that can be observed from Earth—which is called the observable universe. With the eyes alone,

astronomers can see just a small part of the universe. With a small telescope, astronomers can see much farther. With modern telescopes, they can see millions upon millions of miles of the universe.

Distances in space are so vast that it is not practical to measure them in miles or kilometers. The distance to the nearest star, called Proxima Centauri, is more than 25 trillion miles (40 trillion kilometers). The star is so far away that its light, traveling at 186,000 miles (300,000 kilometers) per second, takes more than four years to reach Earth. Therefore, Proxima Centauri is said to be more than four light-years away, four times the distance light travels in one year. The light-year is a convenient unit for measuring distances in space. Astronomers now know of strange bodies, called quasars, that exist at distances of more than 15 billion light-years from Earth.

Using the light-year as a scale, one can get a better idea of the relative distances between, and the sizes of, objects in space. For example, the distance between Earth and the Sun is about 8 light-minutes, and the solar system itself is 11 light-hours across. The brightest star in the sky, called Sirius, is nearly 9 light-years from Earth. The Milky Way galaxy, of which the solar system is a part, is 100,000 light-years across, while the nearest galaxy is 170,000 light-years away.

There is another way of thinking about distances in space. When astronomers look at a star, they do not see the star as it is now. Because the star's rays takes a certain amount of time to travel to Earth, astronomers see them as they were when they were leaving. So, astronomers observe Sirius as it was nine years ago. The most distant quasars are observed as they were 15 billion years ago—not long after the universe itself came into existence.

The big bang theory

How did astronomers determine when the universe began? As their starting point, they used Hubble's idea of an expanding universe. By estimating the rate of expansion, astronomers went backward in time to the moment when the expansion started. Astronomers have calculated that this was between about 15 and 20 billion years ago.

Astronomers think that the universe was born in a fantastic explosion, called the "big bang." The idea of such a primeval explosion was first put forward by Belgian astronomer Georges-Henri Lemaître (1894–1966) in 1927, following the discovery of the outward rush of the galaxies by Hubble.

In line with this theory, it is not possible to speak about a time "before" the big bang because nothing existed—no matter, no space, and no time. For most people, this idea is difficult to imagine. Other ideas about the creation of the universe are equally difficult to grasp.

Scientists think that at the moment of creation, all the matter in the universe was packed into an infinitely small space, and the temperature of this matter was infinitely high. According to the big bang theory, the infinitely dense, infinitely hot fireball of matter exploded to create the expanding universe. As it did so, it started to cool down. In time, clouds of matter (mainly hydrogen gas; H_2) started to clump together under the force of gravity. The clouds grew smaller and denser and began to condense into globes. As these globes collapsed under gravity, they began to heat up again. Eventually, the temperature at their centers reached millions of degrees Fahrenheit. This was hot enough to set off fusion reactions, in which hydrogen atoms fused to form helium atoms. Vast amounts of energy were released, which made the globes glow like stars. In short, the galaxies were born. As the expansion of the universe continued, the galaxies flew farther and farther apart, and they continue to do so.

Measuring the expansion

Astronomers measure the expansion of the universe from the Doppler shift of the light from remote galaxies and quasars. The Doppler shift is the light-wave equivalent of the way sound waves change in pitch when the source of a sound moves away from the listener. A police siren is a familiar example. In the case of galaxies, the fainter the object, the faster it appears to be moving away from Earth.

However, these space objects are not just moving away from Earth. Each object is moving away from every other object. Cosmologists have spent much time trying to calculate the exact rate of expansion.

◀ *Arno Penzias (left) and Robert Wilson (right) won the Nobel Prize for physics for their discovery of the background radiation that provided the first strong evidence in support of the big bang theory.*

These always reach the same peak brightness. Because they are so bright, they can be seen one thousand times farther away than Cepheids.

In 1992, astronomers used the Hubble Space Telescope (HST) to observe Cepheids in a galaxy 16 million light-years away. From this observation, they could link the distance scales found by the two methods mentioned. This produced a Hubble constant of about 45, making the universe at least 14 billion years old.

Work by other astronomers, using stars in the same galaxy, resulted in a Hubble constant of about 80, making the universe younger. This theory causes a problem. The oldest stars are thought to be about 15 billion years old, so if the universe is younger, ideas about the age of stars may be wrong. Some astronomers think that the Doppler shift of distant galaxies may not be caused by the expansion of the universe alone. If this is true, galaxies are not as distant as they appear to be.

This is called the Hubble constant, and it is measured in units of kilometers per second per megaparsec. The Doppler shift of an object is given in kilometers per second, and its distance is given in megaparsecs. One megaparsec is 3.26 million light-years (around 20 billion billion miles).

The Hubble constant is not known accurately. It probably lies between 40 and 80 kilometers per second per megaparsec, making the universe between 10 and 20 billion years old. The reason for the uncertainty is that it can be difficult to measure the distance to remote galaxies. Different methods give different results.

Measuring cosmic distances

The only way to calculate the distance of such remote objects is to look for standard objects nearby whose brightness or size is known. To calculate the distance of galaxies, astronomers look for nearby gas clouds or for stars called Cepheids, which vary in brightness. The brighter the Cepheid, the quicker its brightness varies. Once the rate of variation is measured, the true brightness can be calculated. Comparing this with the brightness as it appears indicates the distance of the Cepheid.

At greater distances, exploding stars, called supernovas, are used to measure cosmic distances.

Fireball radiation

There is convincing evidence for the big bang theory. At the beginning, the universe consisted of a very hot, dense mixture of particles and radiation. The radiation filled all space and gave it an overall temperature. As the universe and space expanded, the radiation became more feeble as it spread out farther, and the temperature of space cooled.

If the big bang theory is correct, there should be some background radiation leftover from the explosion. In 1965, U.S. astronomers Arno Penzias (1933–) and Robert Wilson (1936–) were testing a radio telescope at Holmdel, New Jersey. During their tests, they detected a background noise in the instrument when they tuned in at wavelengths of a few centimeters. This noise, which came from all parts of the sky, turned out to be the background, or fireball, radiation, presumably leftover from the big bang explosion.

Fireball radiation is seen as proof that the universe was once hot and dense, but it has brought problems of its own. If the radiation is from such an early time, why is it so evenly spread? There should be an uneven distribution where the first galaxies were beginning to form. One solution to this question was proposed in 1980 by U.S. astronomer Alan Guth (1947–), who suggested that the early universe expanded rapidly, in what has been called "inflation."

In 1992, excited astronomers announced that the Cosmic Background Explorer (COBE) satellite had detected slight ripples in the smooth background. Cosmologists need to explain how these slight ripples could have eventually turned into the clusters of galaxies that we now see.

Different ideas

Before the discovery of fireball radiation, another theory about the universe was widely held. Called the steady-state theory, it was proposed in 1948 by Austrian-born British mathematician and cosmologist Hermann Bondi (1919–), Austrian-born British astronomer Thomas Gold (1920–2004), and English astronomer and mathematician Fred Hoyle (1915–2001). Steady-state theory did not accept that the universe had a beginning—the universe has always existed and will always remain in the same "steady state." Because the universe is expanding, matter must be created continuously to keep this steady state. Then came the discovery of fireball radiation. Steady-state theory had no explanation for it, but the big bang theory did.

Although most astronomers now agree on how the universe began, they are uncertain about many other ideas. For example, they do not know if the universe is "open" or "closed." In their theories about the nature of the universe, astronomers have found that two kinds of universe are possible. The open universe is one that goes on and on forever. No matter how far one could travel in the universe, one would never reach the end of it.

▶ *This Chandra X-ray Observatory image shows two young galaxies merging, which is providing fuel for the growth of the galaxies' two central black holes (inset).*

The closed universe is more difficult to understand. It is a kind of space that somehow closes in upon itself. A person starting off in one direction would eventually return to the starting point from the other direction. This would be like traveling in a straight line across the surface of Earth because Earth is round. In a closed universe, space is somehow curved.

The death of the universe

Astronomers are also uncertain about how the universe will end, or even if it will end. Theories depend on whether the expansion of the universe continues or will one day stop due to gravity.

If the combined gravity of all the matter in the universe is strong enough, then eventually the galaxies might stop moving outward and begin to retrace their paths through space. The universe would start contracting, the galaxies would get closer together, and space would get hotter and hotter. In perhaps about 150 billion years, what has been called the "big crunch" would come. All the matter in the universe would be squeezed into an infinitely small space and would be at an infinitely high temperature, just as it was at the beginning. Another big bang might then occur, and a new universe might be created. Perhaps it would be made up of different kinds of matter and have different forces and different physical laws from the present universe. This concept is known as the oscillating universe.

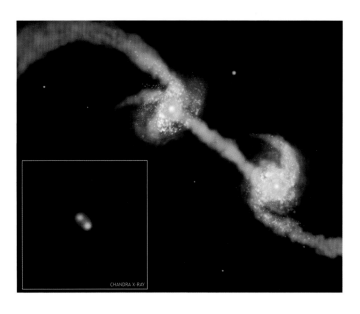

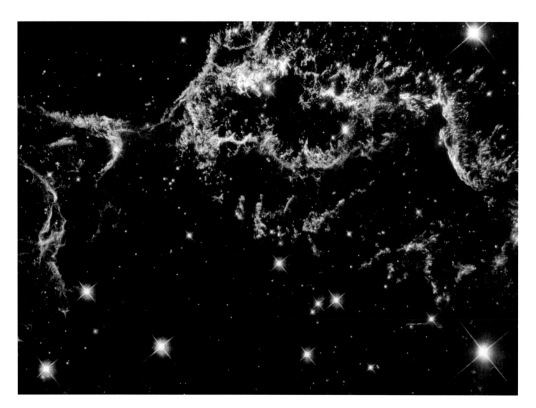

◄ *The expanding debris cloud called Cassiopeia A is an example of the final phase of the life cycle of a star. Light from the explosion that created this supernova remnant was probably first seen in Earth's sky more than three hundred years ago, although it took the light more than 10,000 years to reach Earth.*

Is there enough matter in the universe to make gravity powerful enough to stop the expansion? Astronomers can tell how much material, or mass, there is around distant objects by observing their motions. It looks as if there is up to one hundred times more mass than can be accounted for by the objects that can be seen. This mystery is referred to as the "missing mass" problem.

Astronomers think that there is ten times as much invisible matter as there is visible matter and are searching for the missing mass. It could be ordinary matter that is just invisible (such as dim, cold, or dead stars), or maybe chunks of planet material, or black holes, or particles that have not yet been discovered. Black holes are objects so massive that nothing can escape from them. A black hole containing as much mass as a planet may not be easy to detect.

There may be types of particles that hardly ever affect ordinary matter, which could mean that there are billions of them everywhere, yet we never notice them. One such particle is known—the neutrino. Until 1998, most physicists believed that neutrinos had no mass. Following observations of so-called "neutrino oscillations," physicists now agree that they have a tiny mass, but probably not enough to

make a huge difference. Other suggested particles are called weakly interacting massive particles (WIMPS), but none of them has yet been observed.

So how then will the universe end? It will probably continue to expand and, if so, the stars in all the galaxies would eventually die. The most massive would collapse into black holes. Eventually, most of the matter in each galaxy would collapse into a super black hole, while the rest would be flung out into space. In about 10^{30} (a nonillion) years, the universe would consist of black holes separated by space containing specks of matter.

Finally, it is thought that the particles that make up the nuclei of atoms, protons and neutrons, would break down into a mixture of electrons and positrons (positively charged electrons). The matter in black holes would also eventually turn into these particles. In perhaps 10^{100} years, the universe would be a limitless ocean of widely separated electrons and positrons.

See also: BLACK HOLE • EARTH • NEBULA • NOVA AND SUPERNOVA • RADIOACTIVITY • SOLAR SYSTEM • STAR • SUN

Uranium

The radioactive metal uranium is found in many parts of the world. Before the nineteenth century, there was little use for uranium. However, because it plays an important part in generating nuclear power, uranium has become quite valuable.

Uranium was discovered in 1789 by German chemist Martin Heinrich Klaproth (1743–1817.) He extracted it from a substance called pitchblende, which he found in the mountains of a country then known as Bohemia (now the Czech Republic). Uranium was not considered a useful substance, except that its compounds—which are often beautiful shades of yellow and orange—were used to color glass and as glazes for ceramics.

Radioactivity

In the late 1890s, scientists became aware that uranium compounds blackened photographic paper. This was the first time anyone had observed the effects of radioactivity.

A substance is radioactive when the atoms making up the substance release particles and gradually change their chemical identity as they do so. In the case of uranium, the material releases particles known as alpha particles. Over a long period, the uranium changes from one radioactive material to another, and it finally ends up as lead.

As this happens, the uranium releases energy. Scientists had knowledge of this for many years, but because the process was so slow, they did not think there was any way the energy could be harnessed. However, developments in the twentieth century revealed that the process could be sped up and the energy could be used either to provide heat in nuclear power stations or to make weapons.

Where it is found

Uranium is now so widely used that it has become an important resource for countries that export it. Uranium ores (rocks containing uranium compounds) are found in Zaire in central Africa, and Namibia in southern Africa, as well as in Australia, Canada, parts of Europe, South America, the United States, and many other countries. Prospectors locate the uranium deposits using Geiger-Müller detectors, which are devices for detecting the presence of radioactive materials.

Uranium ore is mined in one of two ways. The open-pit method is simply to dig a large hole in the ground and recover the ore. The other technique is deep-mining, which means people must work underground. In both methods, but especially when working underground, miners have to be careful not to inhale the radioactive dust because it can cause cancer or otherwise damage their health.

Once mined, the ore is crushed and the uranium itself is separated from the ore with a strong alkali or acid. After further processing, the result is a yellow material, called yellow cake, which contains about 50 percent uranium oxide (UO_2).

▶ *This is a sample of the black mineral uraninite (uranium oxide) and yellowish-brown gummite (uranium hydroxide). Uraninite is usually found in this form, mixed with other compounds of uranium, when it is known as pitchblende.*

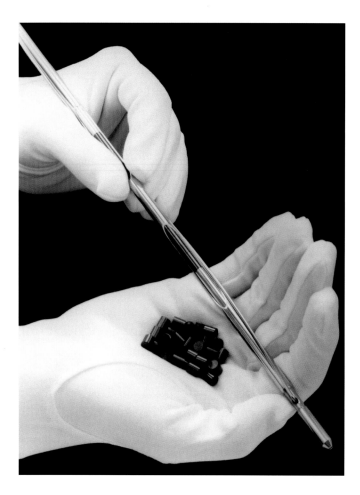

These are nuclear fuel pellets with their injection rod. Each pellet can produce the same amount of energy as 3 tons (3 tonnes) of coal. The pellets are designed for use in fast breeder nuclear reactors.

Nuclear fission

Uranium consists of two isotopes of uranium, called uranium-238 and uranium-235. Only about 0.73 percent of uranium as it occurs naturally is the uranium-235 isotope. The rest is uranium-238.

Uranium-235 is the only natural material that will undergo nuclear fission when it is struck by a slow-moving neutron. Such materials are called fissile. At the center of each uranium atom—and all other atoms—there is a nucleus composed of particles called protons and neutrons. If a neutron strikes the nucleus of a uranium-235 atom, the nucleus will split into two lighter nuclei. This is nuclear fission. As it happens, neutrons are released from the nucleus, and this sets up a chain reaction of further fission.

Nuclear fission creates an enormous amount of energy in the form of heat. When a nuclear weapon is exploded, the uncontrolled chain reaction creates massive destructive energy. In a power station, the heat produced is used to create the steam or gas that operates the turbines.

Some nuclear power stations use uranium-238 and uranium-235 in the proportions in which they occur naturally, but for most reactors it is necessary to enrich the uranium fuel. This means removing some of the uranium-238, so the proportion of uranium-235 becomes greater, usually about four percent.

The leftover uranium-238 does not undergo fission, but it is still useful. The nucleus of a uranium-238 atom can absorb a neutron and then undergo a series of radioactive changes that lead to the creation of a plutonium atom. Plutonium will undergo fission and can be used to generate heat in a new kind of nuclear reactor called a fast breeder reactor, now in use in some parts of the world.

Refining uranium

Most uranium is mined for eventual use in nuclear reactors, which are the source of heat for nuclear power stations. The proper working of the reactor depends on the uranium being absolutely pure—the smallest amount of impurity can keep the reactor from working. Thorough refining of the uranium is, therefore, important.

The yellow cake is dissolved in nitric acid (HNO_3), and uranyl nitrate ($UO_2(NO_3)_2$) is formed. This goes through various processes to become pure uranium oxide, which is made into pellets and sealed in protective cans to form the fuel elements in a nuclear reactor. (Some designs of reactor, particularly in Britain and Canada, use other compounds of uranium as fuel elements.)

The material is put into cans to prevent it from reacting with the gas or liquid used to carry the heat produced from this fuel to the turbines (which generate electricity). The cans also help keep radioactivity from escaping into the air.

See also: ATOM AND MOLECULE • GEIGER-MÜLLER DETECTOR • RADIOACTIVITY

Uranus

Uranus is the third largest planet in the solar system; only Jupiter and Saturn are larger. Uranus is too far away to be seen from Earth with the naked eye. Even through the most powerful telescopes, Uranus appears as no more than a pale greenish disk, with faint markings (probably "wind belts") on either side of its equator.

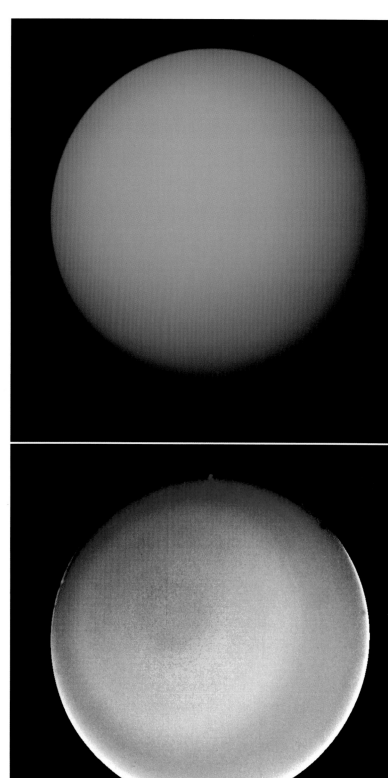

Uranus is so remote and faint that it remained undiscovered until March 13, 1781, when German-born British astronomer William Herschel (1738–1822) spotted what he first thought was a comet. When the orbit was calculated, however, the "comet" turned out to be another planet. Herschel named the planet Georgium Sidus in honor of his patron, King George III (1738–1820) of England. Eventually, it was renamed Uranus according to the tradition of naming planets for the gods of Greek and Roman mythology.

Unusual Uranus

Uranus is the seventh planet in order of increasing distance from the Sun, and lies beyond Saturn. On average, Uranus orbits 1.7 billion miles (2.8 billion kilometers) from the Sun, taking 84 years to make one complete orbit. The planet has a diameter of more than 32,000 miles (52,000 kilometers)—just a fraction larger than Neptune but roughly four times the diameter of Earth. The volume of Uranus is around 62 times Earth's volume. However, the density of Uranus (80 pounds per cubic foot or 1,285 kilograms per cubic meter), which is a

▶ These two pictures of Uranus—one in true color (top) and the other in false color—were rendered using images returned on January 17, 1986, by the Voyager 2 space probe. Voyager 2 was 9.1 million kilometers (5.7 million miles) from the planet when the pictures were taken.

◄ **This composite image of Ariel, a moon of Uranus, was taken by the Voyager 2 spacecraft on January 24, 1986. The image reveals small impact craters on the surface of Ariel, as well as evidence of geological activity in the form of numerous valleys, faults, and fractures.**

DID YOU KNOW?

William Herschel was born in Hanover, Germany on November 15, 1738. After brief military service, Herschel moved to Bath, England, and became a successful musician. At the same time, he pursued an interest in astronomy. With the help of his sister Caroline, Herschel started to record objects in the night sky using telescopes he built himself. Although the discovery of Uranus is Herschel's most famous achievement, he also discovered the outer two Uranian satellites, Titania and Oberon, in 1787. Herschel also made many important observations of stars and nebulas, which led to revolutionary ideas about the nature of the universe. His theory that nebulas were clusters of stars moving through space anticipated later ideas about the expansion of the universe.

measure of the mass per volume, is only one-fourth the density of Earth. The difference is due to the composition of Uranus. Unlike Earth, Uranus consists of a large proportion of gas and ice and a relatively small proportion of rock. Indeed, only the core of the planet is thought to be composed of rock, which is probably lightweight iron-rich silicates. The overlying mantle is likely to consist of frozen water, methane (CH_4), and some ammonia (NH_3). The deep layer of clouds that make up the planet's atmosphere largely consists of hydrogen and helium, but there is a small amount of methane, which gives Uranus its blue-green color.

Cool planet

If an astronaut could travel to Uranus, he or she would find conditions on the planet unbearably cold. Because there is little heat generated by the interior of the planet, Uranus relies on the Sun for warmth. Given the vast distance between Uranus and the Sun, it is no surprise that the temperature of Uranus's atmosphere is a chilly −353°F (−214°C).

The tilting axis

Like all the other planets, Uranus rotates on its axis while orbiting the Sun. Uranus rotates once every 16 hours. Unlike the other planets, however, its axis of rotation is highly tilted, that is, Uranus spins on its side. This unusual tilt means that the plane of the planet's equator is more or less at right angles to the plane of the planet's orbit. As a result, the days and seasons on Uranus are not like those on Earth. As Uranus orbits the Sun, the north and south poles of the planet alternately point toward the Sun. Because the orbital period is 84 years, the summer season, which corresponds to one Earth day, lasts for 42 Earth years, and the winter season, which corresponds to one Earth night, lasts for another 42 Earth years.

Data from *Voyager 2*

In January 1986, data sent back to Earth from the *Voyager 2* space probe gave astronomers more detailed knowledge of Uranus than had existed since its discovery in 1781. That day, *Voyager 2* flew within 50,679 miles (81,560 kilometers) of Uranus, which is a relatively close encounter in outer space. Uranus was known to have nine rings, but images from the space probe revealed two more. The

▶ *The ring system around Uranus, shown in this picture taken by the Hubble Space Telescope, was discovered in 1977 by observing a star passing by the planet. The star was seen to "blink" briefly five times before the planet and again five times afterward, revealing that Uranus was encircled by five narrow rings. Astronomers are now aware of 11 rings in the system.*

▲ *This false-color photograph of the ring system of Uranus was taken by the* **Voyager 2** *spacecraft on January 21, 1986. The mission revealed the existence of 11 separate rings and also showed that the rings are surrounded by belts of fine dust.*

images also showed the rings were mostly boulder-sized chunks of dark material. Astronomers now think that the rings consist of ice and rock debris leftover from a collision.

Also, the five known moons orbiting Uranus were increased to 15 when *Voyager 2* took photographs of ten smaller moons, ranging from 25 to 43 miles (40 to 70 kilometers) in diameter. The five largest moons—Miranda, Ariel, Umbriel, Oberon, and Titania—range from 200 miles (320 kilometers) to 650 miles (1,046 kilometers) across.

Astronomers think that the five largest moons consist primarily of ice and silicate rocks. The surface of all the main moons are littered with impact craters. Oberon and Umbriel appear to have old impact craters that could possibly date back to collisions during the formation of the solar system.

Titania and Ariel have smaller craters that must have been produced more recently. *Voyager 2* photographs showed features such as faults, fractures, and valleys—evidence of geological activity that would have removed the older craters on Titania and Ariel.

Data from *Voyager 2* also showed that the magnetic field on Uranus differs from nearly all other planets. Uranus has a strong magnetic field generated by the movement of ionized atoms within the liquid mantle. Unusually, the north and south magnetic poles are each 30 degrees from its equator, rather than being close to its rotation axis. Astronomers do not know why the magnetic field exhibits this dramatic tilt. Perhaps Uranus is in the middle of a reversal of the north and south poles, or it could even be that a past collision with a large body has disoriented the magnetic field.

See also: JUPITER • NEPTUNE • SATURN • SOLAR SYSTEM

Vaccination

Vaccination prevents people from getting diseases. A person being vaccinated is given dead or very weak versions of germ cells. This makes the body build up antibodies—its defenses against the germs. Later, the body will be able to use the antibodies to kill any live germs that try to invade it.

In a vaccination, a person is given a substance called a vaccine, which can be introduced into the body by injection or by mouth. The vaccine contains the bacterium or virus that causes a particular disease. The presence of this foreign matter in the person's body causes the immune system to fight it—just as it does whenever disease-causing germs invade the body. As a result, the body builds up defenses in the form of antibodies, which are special protein substances that give the person immunity against that particular organism. In this way, the person cannot later be affected by the disease.

If vaccination were given with highly infectious bacteria or viruses, the person would get the very disease that the vaccination was supposed to prevent. Instead, a vaccine consists of dead bacteria or viruses, or of microorganisms that have been weakened and are no longer dangerous.

The first vaccinations

In the late eighteenth century, English physician Edward Jenner (1749–1823) noticed that milkmaids who had cowpox (a fairly mild disease) seemed to be protected against smallpox—a disease that killed many people each year at that time. Jenner decided to give people cowpox artificially to see if it would protect them from catching smallpox.

To do this, Jenner injected the fluid from the sores caused by cowpox into people who were at risk of catching smallpox. As a result, Jenner discovered that his patients were protected against smallpox. The cowpox fluid worked because the

▼ *Vaccination against smallpox, using a kit such as the one in the picture below, has been a worldwide success. In 1979, the World Health Organization (WHO) declared smallpox to be extinct.*

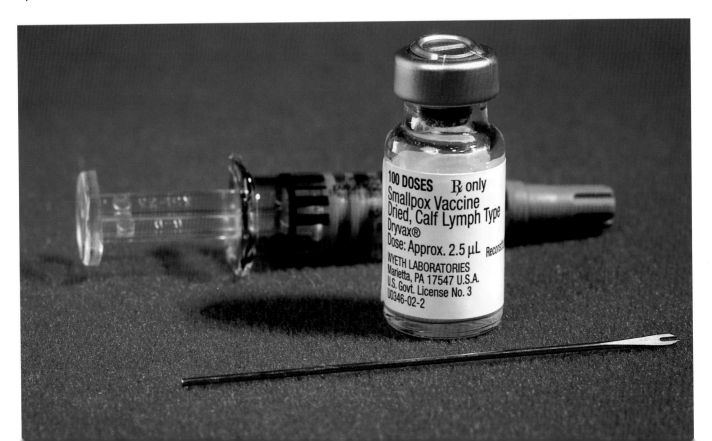

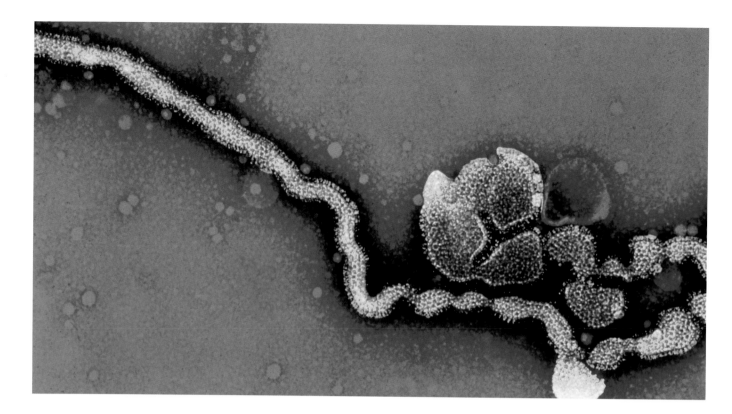

▲ *This electron-microscope image shows an influenza type C virus. Influenza viruses are divided into types—A, B, or C. Types A and B are dangerous, and scientists try to create vaccines for them. Type C causes only mild illness, similar to the common cold, so no vaccine has been developed.*

cowpox virus was similar to the smallpox virus. The defense the body built up against cowpox worked equally well against smallpox. The technique Jenner used was called vaccination after the vaccinia virus, which is the scientific name for the cowpox virus.

How does a vaccination work?

The body reacts to infecting microorganisms, also called microbes, in two ways. It produces chemicals called antibodies that destroy the microbes. It also produces cells that can later "remember" the particular type of infecting microbe if there is a second infection. These cells cluster around the microbes and attract other cells, which swallow up the infecting microorganisms. This reaction is called cell-mediated immunity.

A vaccination is given to make the immune system think it is being infected with a disease. The two defenses against that specific microbe—

antibodies and cell-mediated immunity—are therefore set up. If the person later comes in contact with the same microbe, the body's defenses are present to destroy any that might enter the body.

Live vaccines

The most effective vaccines are those that contain live viruses or bacteria. However, it is not possible to inject the dangerous organism in its usual form. If this were done, people would catch the disease itself. Instead, the virus or bacterium must be treated so that it is "safe" or weakened. This is done by growing the microbes for many generations under strictly controlled conditions. In these conditions, the microbes slowly lose their ability to cause disease, although they keep their ability to activate the body's immune system.

When these weakened microbes are given in the form of a vaccination, they grow inside the body, and the body's defenses are built up against them. Because they are weakened, though, the microbes do not produce the symptoms of the disease.

The polio vaccine (Sabin vaccine) is a good example of weakened-virus vaccine. The vaccine is made from weakened polio virus that was first cultivated in the 1950s. The vaccine is not injected but is given orally because the polio virus normally infects a person through the mouth and then the intestines. Giving the vaccine by mouth therefore stimulates the body's defenses where they are needed most—in the wall of the intestines.

Dead vaccines

In some cases, it is not possible to produce a weakened form of the virus or bacterium. To obtain a vaccine, the bacteria or viruses are first grown in large quantities and are then carefully killed. These killed microbes are then processed and an extract taken from the dead microbes is used as a vaccine.

When microbes activate the body's defenses, chemicals called antigens (distinguishing chemicals) on the surface of the bacterium or virus cause antibodies and cell-mediated immunity to be produced. A vaccine made from dead microbes contains these surface antigens, and it therefore causes the body to set up its defenses.

These dead vaccines involve less risk than live vaccines because there are no infecting microorganisms growing in the body. However, two doses of dead vaccine must be given. The first dose causes the body to produce fairly small amounts of the defense cells, and these do not last long. However, the second dose, called a booster, results in a much larger production of antibody and cell-mediated immunity and sets up the immune system to cope with any infection by the live form of the bacterium or virus.

The end of smallpox

The development of the vaccinia vaccination against smallpox resulted in the greatest success story for vaccination thus far. At one time, smallpox was the most feared human disease. Many people died of this infection, and those who survived were often severely scarred.

In the twentieth century, large-scale vaccination campaigns were started, and smallpox gradually disappeared from Europe and North America. Anyone traveling outside these areas had to be

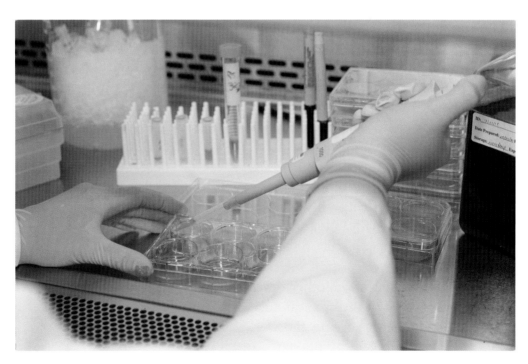

▶ *This scientist is seeding petri dishes with weakened virus cells to test the vaccine ChimeriVax-JE, a vaccine that is being developed to protect against the Japanese encephalitis (JE) virus. This dangerous virus can cause paralysis, coma, and death.*

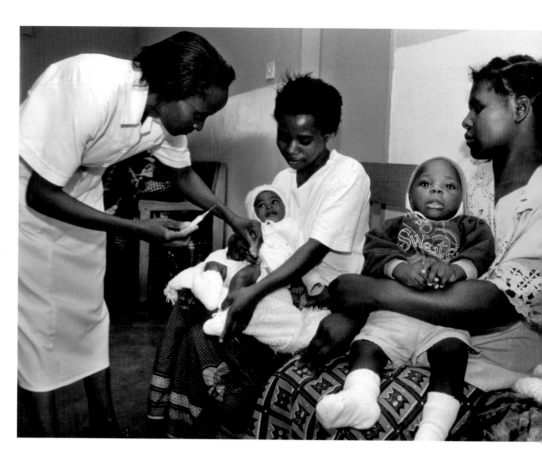

▶ *This nurse in a community clinic in Lusaka, Zambia, is giving DTP vaccinations to babies. This vaccine protects them against diphtheria, tetanus, and pertussis (whooping cough). Vaccination is a low-cost way to prevent infectious diseases, and vaccination programs have had a huge impact on improving world health.*

vaccinated, and vaccination campaigns were started in more and more countries. Fewer and fewer people caught the disease and, in 1980, the World Health Organization (WHO) officially declared the disease to be eradicated.

Colds and influenza

There is only one type of smallpox virus, so only one type of vaccine had to be developed. The viruses that cause common colds and influenza are at the other extreme; there are hundreds of different types, called variants, of the same virus. Each variant has different antigens on its surface. A vaccine produced against one antigenic type would not protect against all the other antigenic types.

With the common cold, this problem has not been overcome, but with influenza there has been some success. There is usually only one antigenic type of flu virus in circulation each year. As one antigenic type disappears, another develops to fill its place. The WHO keeps a careful watch on outbreaks of influenza around the world, and as soon as a new antigenic type starts to spread,

scientists work to develop a vaccine for it. This vaccine can then be used by people in many different countries before the new virus reaches them.

Vaccines for cancer

No single vaccine would be able to prevent cancer. A vaccine can only build up the body's defenses against invading microbes such as bacteria and viruses. It is suspected that viruses are in some way involved in producing cancers, but the link is not easy to prove.

However, one virus—the Epstein-Barr virus—has definitely been linked to a rare cancer of the nose, throat, and neck. Much research is being done to develop a vaccine to use against the Epstein-Barr virus, but it is difficult to obtain the antigenic chemicals from the virus in pure form. Without these chemicals, it is impossible to produce an effective vaccine.

See also: BACTERIA • DRUG INDUSTRY • VIRUS, BIOLOGICAL

Vacuum

A vacuum is a space that is empty of matter. An absolute vacuum—the total absence of matter—is not known to exist, so a vacuum is a space with a pressure less than atmospheric pressure. Vacuums are used in food preparation, nuclear research, and science and industry.

A vacuum is made with a system of pumps that remove the air from a space. A vacuum can range from low to ultrahigh, which is many millionths of atmospheric pressure. The amount of vacuum is measured in units of pressure. These units are either the torr (millimeters of mercury) or pascals, the Système International (SI) unit. Standard atmospheric pressure is 760 torr or 101,325 pascals, so 1 torr is about 133 pascals.

Oil-sealed rotary pumps

This type of vacuum pump is widely used and works by compressing (squeezing together) a volume of air until the pressure is high enough for the air to force its way out of an exhaust valve in the pump. If the exhaust pressure is not high enough, a second-stage pump can be used to compress the air further. One pump can reach a vacuum of 5 pascals. A two-stage pump can produce vacuums as high as 0.5 pascal.

Vapor diffusion pump

Diffusion pumps do not actively "pull" air molecules out of a volume; rather, they wait for the molecules to diffuse into the active part of the pump, where they are trapped and then removed.

Vapor diffusion pumps are used to reach the very highest vacuums of more than 10^{-9} pascals. This type of ultrahigh vacuum is not necessary for most purposes, and these pumps are usually used to produce vacuums of about 10^{-4} pascals (about

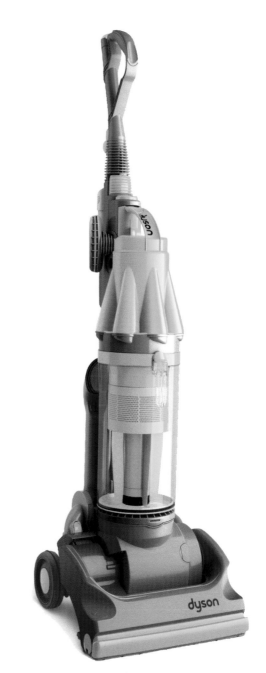

▲ *Vacuum cleaners, such as this one, produce a partial vacuum, which they use to suck up dust and other small particles from the floor.*

one-billionth of an atmosphere). Vapor diffusion pumps only work at pressures below 10 pascals, so they are usually used with a rotary pump.

A vapor diffusion pump operates by boiling oil at the base of the pump. As the hot oil vapor rises, it is directed into a funnel-shaped set of baffles (known as a chimney stack) and jetted as a supersonic vapor toward the sides, which are kept cool by coils of tubing containing cold water. Air molecules that diffuse into this portion of the pump collide with the vapor molecules and are

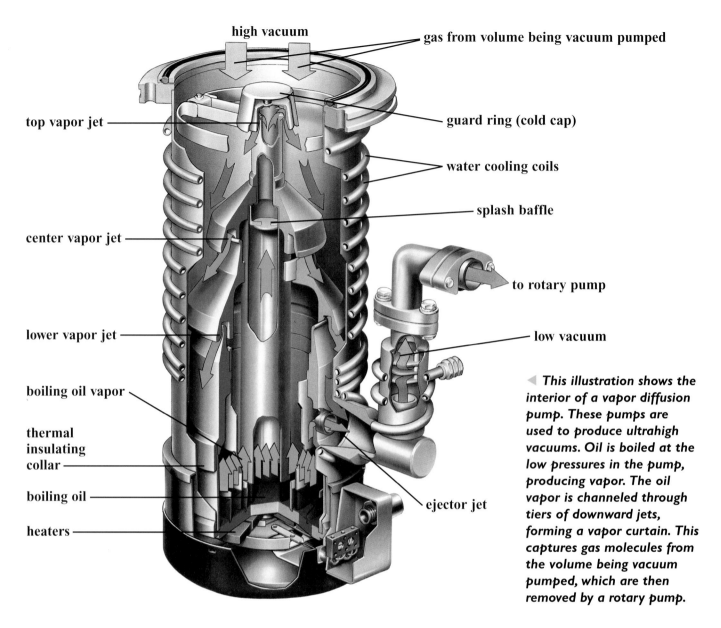

high vacuum

gas from volume being vacuum pumped

top vapor jet

guard ring (cold cap)

water cooling coils

splash baffle

center vapor jet

to rotary pump

lower vapor jet

low vacuum

boiling oil vapor

thermal insulating collar

boiling oil

heaters

ejector jet

◀ *This illustration shows the interior of a vapor diffusion pump. These pumps are used to produce ultrahigh vacuums. Oil is boiled at the low pressures in the pump, producing vapor. The oil vapor is channeled through tiers of downward jets, forming a vapor curtain. This captures gas molecules from the volume being vacuum pumped, which are then removed by a rotary pump.*

trapped. The oil vapor cools and condenses, dragging air molecules down as it sinks to the bottom of the pump. At the bottom, the heater reboils the oil, releasing the air molecules, which are pumped away by the rotary pump.

Making use of vacuums

Some vacuums, such as those used in vacuum-lifting equipment, need only be between 1,000 and 10,000 pascals. Other vacuums, such as those required in high-energy particle storage rings used in nuclear research, need to be ultrahigh—about 10^{-8} pascals. There are so few air molecules left in a vacuum this high that one molecule has to travel about 300 miles (500 kilometers) before it collides

with another air molecule. Some devices use this principle of a long path before a collision. They include vacuum coating, particle accelerators, and television picture tubes.

Vacuum coating is a process used to manufacture everyday items such as camera lenses, water faucets, headlight reflectors for automobiles, and bottle tops. A rotary pump and a vapor diffusion pump are used together to create a vacuum of about 0.001 pascal. The material to form the coating, such as aluminum, is heated as a filament (a fine wire heated by passing an electrical current through it). When the filament gets hot enough, the aluminum evaporates (turn to vapor) and then condenses back to a solid state on the cool surface to be

▶ *Reflective metal coating is applied to automobile headlights as a vapor in a vacuum coating chamber.*

coated. Because there are virtually no air molecules to get in the way of this process, the aluminum is deposited as a clean, smooth, uniform film.

Vacuums are also used in freeze-drying equipment. The process of freeze-drying removes water from food. This process is used in the production of some instant coffee, in food processing, and in producing vaccines and other pharmaceutical products.

Vacuum cleaners

Vacuum cleaners get their name because they make use of a partial vacuum to draw up dirt and dust. The electrically powered fan unit creates an airstream that moves at high speed through a pick-up nozzle. As the fan rotates, air is sent out from the edges of the nozzle, and this creates a partial vacuum at the center of the fan. Air containing the dust and dirt from the surroundings is then drawn up through the nozzle to fill the vacuum.

The first vacuum cleaner was patented by English engineer Hubert Cecil Booth (1871–1955) in 1901. It used a 5-horsepower piston engine. Modern vacuum cleaners usually operate with an electric fan unit, which causes a strong airstream, drawing up air through the nozzle (cleaning head). The efficiency of the cleaner depends on the size of the fan and the design of the blades, as well as the strength of the electric motor driving the fan.

Vacuum flask

Another everyday object that makes use of a vacuum is the vacuum, or thermos, flask. It was invented by Scottish chemist and physicist James Dewar (1842–1923) in the 1890s. Dewar used it to store liquid gases at low temperatures. The vacuum flask works by thermally insulating its contents to keep heat from flowing in or out.

The flask is a glass vessel with double walls. The glass is silvered (similar to a mirror) to reduce infrared (heat) radiation. The space between the walls is a vacuum. The combination of the silvering and the vacuum reduces heat transfer by convection, conduction, and radiation. Vacuum flasks can therefore keep hot liquids hot and cold liquids cold. Because the glass vessel is so fragile, it is usually mounted on pads of cork or rubber inside a plastic or metal container for protection.

See also: PRESSURE • PUMP

Valence

Elements make up all forms of matter on Earth. Elements may be solid, liquid, or gas, and they combine with each other to make compounds. Each element has a valence number, which informs chemists about its ability to combine with other elements.

Elements consist of tiny particles called atoms. When one element (A) combines with another element (B) to form a compound, the atoms of A bond with the atoms of B. Units formed by groups of atoms are called molecules.

Molecules

Different molecules contain different numbers of atoms. Water contains two hydrogen atoms and one oxygen atom (H_2O). Table salt contains one sodium atom and one chlorine atom (NaCl).

The number of atoms in a molecule depends on the valence of each atom. An atom's valence is its ability to combine with other atoms. This can be thought of as the number of chemical bonds the atom can make with other atoms.

Scientists first figured out that elements have valency in the middle of the nineteenth century. They realized that each hydrogen atom can make only one bond, so hydrogen has a valence of 1. From there, they worked out all the other valences by making a simple calculation. Water has one oxygen atom and two hydrogen atoms in each molecule, so oxygen must have a valence of 2.

Valence electrons

It is not necessary to figure out an element's valence on the basis of combinations with hydrogen atoms. Chemists look at the structure of the atom itself.

Each atom has a nucleus (center) surrounded by shells (layers) of electrons. The shell nearest the nucleus is full when it contains two electrons. The

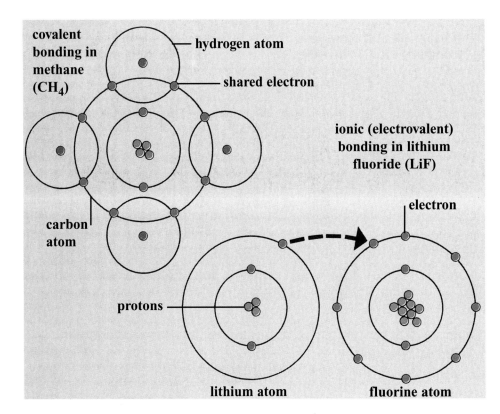

covalent bonding in methane (CH_4)

hydrogen atom

shared electron

carbon atom

ionic (electrovalent) bonding in lithium fluoride (LiF)

electron

protons

lithium atom

fluorine atom

◄ *Methane (above left) is formed by covalent bonding between one carbon atom and four hydrogen atoms. Sharing the atoms in their outer shells fills both outer shells of each element. Lithium fluoride (below right) is formed by ionic bonding. The one electron in the outer shell of the lithium atom is transferred to the fluorine atom, giving them both complete outer shells. Losing one electron gives the lithium atom a positive charge, and it becomes a lithium ion. By gaining an atom, the fluorine becomes negatively charged. Because positive and negative charges attract, the two ions form an ionic (also called electrovalent) bond.*

next shell is full when it contains eight electrons. The higher an element is ranked in the periodic table (the chart of the elements), the more electrons it has in each atom. The heaviest known elements (with the most electrons) have seven shells.

A few elements have atoms with full outer shells, but most have incomplete outer shells with fewer than the full number of electrons. The valence of an element depends on the number of electrons in the outer shell of its atom. It is these electrons that form the bonds to make compounds. Atoms with full outer shells do not form bonds easily. When two or more elements form a compound, the bonds they make give them each a full outer shell. There are two types of bonding: ionic and covalent.

Ionic bonding

In an ionic bond, one atom donates one or more electrons from its outer shell to another atom. For example, lithium has one electron in its outer shell. Fluorine has seven. The lithium easily gives up its single electron to the fluorine atom, so both atoms have complete outer shells.

Once the lithium has lost its electron, the atom has one more proton (positive particles in the nucleus) than electrons. So it has a positive charge. The fluorine, having an extra electron, is negatively charged. The two atoms attract each other, and it is this attraction that forms the bond and produces lithium fluoride. Charged atoms are called ions, so the bond they form is called ionic.

Atoms with one, two, or three electrons in their outer shell usually lose electrons. Those with five, six, or seven usually gain them. The valence is equal to the number of electrons lost or gained. These electrons are called valence electrons.

Covalent bonding

In covalent bonding, the electrons are shared between the atoms of a compound. Carbon, which has four electrons in its outer shell, forms covalent bonds. In methane (CH_4), the carbon atom shares each of its outer electrons with a different hydrogen atom. The hydrogen shares its one outer electron with the carbon atom. Therefore, it has an outer shell of two electrons, and the carbon atom has a full outer shell of eight. The valence of the carbon is equal to the number of covalent bonds it makes.

Elements with different valences

All molecules are built up from ionic or covalent bonds. In large molecules, both types of bond are present. Many elements can combine in several different ways and therefore have several valences. For example, sulfur has valences of 2, 4, and 6. It can form both covalent and ionic bonds.

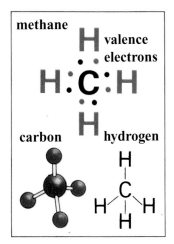

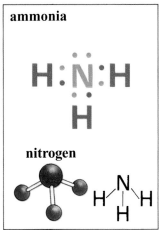

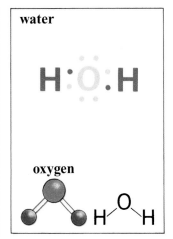

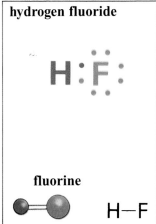

▲ *These hydrogen compounds are all formed by covalent bonds. The electrons in the atoms' outer shells are shared between the atoms.*

See *also*: CHEMICAL REACTION

Valve

A valve is a device that controls the flow or pressure of fluid in a pipe. It does this by opening or closing like a gate or a plug. There are many different types of valves. Some work automatically, but others need an outside force to operate them.

Some valves are quite simple—they work by moving to an open or closed position. Others are more complex. They have moving parts that can adjust the rate of flow of a fluid. Some work on a timing system. There are many different types of valves, but all are either automatic or nonautomatic. Most of the valves described in this article are nonautomatic.

Lift valves

Lift valves must be lifted vertically in and out of position. This is often done by fitting them to a screw that is turned by a wheel or handle. One common example of a lift valve is the stop valve that operates a water faucet.

Stop valves

The stop valve on a faucet is attached to a spindle (long rod). At the top of the spindle is a handle, which turns the faucet on and off. At the other end is a disk that is connected to a washer made from rubber or leather. Water from a water pipe flows into a faucet through an opening called the valve seat. The washer "sits" in the valve seat when the valve is shut.

When the handle of the faucet is turned off, the valve closes, and water cannot pass from the pipe to the faucet. If the handle is turned slightly, the

washer is raised a little, and some water can trickle through. If the faucet is turned on full, the opening is completely clear, and the water can gush out.

Washer replacement

When a washer becomes worn, it does not fit the seat properly, the faucet drips, and it has to be replaced. If a washer becomes shredded, it can damage the soft metal of the seat. However, the separate parts of a stop valve for steam flow are made of metal and are machined for a perfect fit.

Stop valves that are subject to high pressure are shaped so that fluid can flow equally around them, thus reducing wear. They are called balance valves.

▶ This system of gate valves controls the flow of drilling lubricants on an oil rig in the North Sea. The gate valve is one of the most commonly used industrial valves.

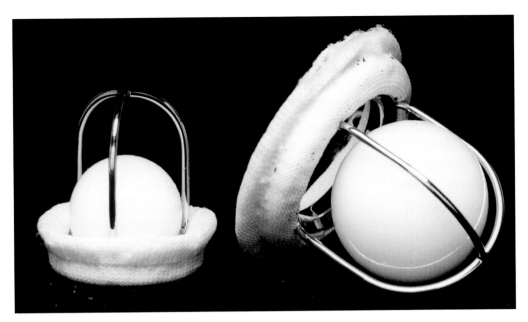

◀ The heart has four valves that control the flow of blood through it. Artificial valves such as these can be implanted if the natural valves fail to function through disease.

Needle valves

The needle valve is another version of the stop valve. Instead of a disk, it has a tapering pin that is inserted into the seat. When it is screwed all the way down, the opening is closed. The needle valve adjusts flow more precisely than an ordinary stop valve. It is often used in the radiator controls of home central-heating systems.

Gate valves

Gate valves are basically lift valves. They are very large, and they are normally used for controlling the flow of liquid in pipelines or water mains.

A gate valve consists of a wedge-shaped gate that is attached to a screw and handle. When the gate is down, it cuts off the flow of water. The gate must be in only one of two positions—either open or shut. If it is partly open, the flow of water is turbulent.

Internal combustion engine valves

Lift valves are also used in internal combustion engines. An intake valve opens to let the air and gas mixture into the cylinder. An exhaust valve opens to let the spent gases out. These valves are machined to make them fit tightly, so fuel is used efficiently. They are operated by a timing gear that drives a camshaft, which presses on a spring attached to the stems of the valves.

Globe valves

The globe valve is so called because it is spherical in shape. This lift valve is used in plumbing to control the flow of liquid around a 90-degree angle.

Valves operated by steam

Steam boilers and hydraulic mechanisms need safety valves. A safety valve is normally held shut by a spring or a weight. If the pressure of steam in a boiler exceeds a safe level, it pushes the valve open. The excess steam is then allowed to escape.

A different type of steam valve is the slide valve on a steam engine cylinder. Slide valves move back and forth, uncovering and covering openings in the cylinder and letting steam in at adjustable intervals. Steam from one direction, and springs from the other, provide the pressure to operate them.

Check valves

The fluid in an automatic valve is controlled without external pressure. An example is the check valve used in pumps to prevent fluid from flowing backward. The valve is a hinged flap or a ball. As the fluid flows toward the flap, its pressure lifts the flap. When it flows back again from the other side, its pressure forces the valve to close again.

See *also:* HYDRAULICS • PUMP

Vapor pressure

When a substance is in a liquid form, molecules are continually escaping from, and returning to, its surface. These escaping molecules form vapor. Vapor exerts an external force, called vapor pressure, on its surroundings.

A gas is called a vapor when its temperature drops below a value called the critical point. Below this temperature, a gas may be liquefied by increasing pressure. Above this temperature, however, a gas may not be liquefied no matter how much pressure is exerted. In the case of water, the critical temperature is 705°F (374°C). The higher the temperature of a vapor, the greater the pressure it exerts, and the harder the vapor must be compressed to turn it into a liquid (condense).

Molecules in a liquid have a certain amount of kinetic energy. The amount of this energy increases with temperature. Some of the molecules at the surface of a liquid will have sufficient energy to escape from the attractive forces of other molecules and thus free themselves from the liquid to become a vapor. This process is known as evaporation. Evaporation occurs continually at the surface of a liquid, so there is always some vapor in contact with the liquid. The temperature at which the pressure exerted by vapor (the vapor pressure) at the surface of a liquid becomes equal to the pressure exerted by the surroundings is called the boiling point.

Vapor pressure depends on temperature only so long as there is some liquid present. Gas pressure, however, depends on the volume of the gas as well as the temperature. If the volume of a gas is increased, the pressure will decrease. If the volume of a vapor is increased, however, the pressure on the surface of the liquid decreases. Thus, more molecules are permitted to escape, and the vapor pressure remains constant.

Saturated and unsaturated vapor

When a gas below its critical temperature is reduced in volume, its pressure increases until it begins to condense. From that point, the vapor pressure remains the same and, if the volume is reduced further, the pressure remains constant while more

▶ *Clouds are formed from water vapor in the atmosphere. As temperature reduces with altitude, moisture high in the air falls below its saturated vapor pressure and condenses into droplets, which appear together as clouds.*

▶ *In the morning, grass is often covered with water droplets called dew. When the ground cools at night, the air in contact with it also cools. As warm air holds more moisture than cold air, some of the water condenses onto the grass.*

liquid condenses. This pressure is called the saturated, or equilibrium, vapor pressure of the substance at that temperature, and it is the maximum pressure the vapor can have. The number of particles leaving the surface is in equilibrium (balance) with those returning to it. The vapor pressure can be reduced if there is no liquid present, in which case the vapor is said to be unsaturated.

The saturated vapor pressure of water at room temperature is 0.02 atmosphere (a unit of pressure equal to the pressure of the air at sea level). If a vacuum pump is attached to a container holding water, the water will start to boil when the pressure falls to the saturated vapor pressure. This is because the liquid rapidly evaporates to keep the pressure at the saturated value. In general, the boiling point of a liquid is the temperature at which the saturated vapor is equal to the pressure of the atmosphere.

The amount of water vapor in the atmosphere can be measured by its vapor pressure, which ranges from saturated in still air in contact with water, to practically zero in deserts. The relative humidity is the ratio of the actual vapor pressure to the saturated vapor pressure at that temperature. Relative humidity is measured using a hygrometer.

Clouds and dew

The dew on grass in the morning is caused by the pressure of water vapor in the air falling below its saturated value. When the ground cools during the night, the air in contact with it also cools. Because cold air can hold less water vapor than warm air, this cooling causes any water vapor in the air to condense, forming droplets of dew. The temperature at which dew forms is called the dew point.

Clouds are formed by a similar process. Warm, moist air rises into cooler upper regions of the atmosphere. At this lower temperature, the moisture content is too great for the air to hold as a vapor, and some of the moisture condenses to form droplets.

The vapor pressure in clouds can become greater than the theoretical saturated vapor pressure. When this happens, the vapor is said to be supersaturated. The water in the vapor will not form into droplets on its own. It needs cores of dust particles or salt crystals around which to condense.

See also: ATMOSPHERE • ATOM AND MOLECULE • CLOUD • PRESSURE • SUBLIMATION • VACUUM • WATER

Venturi effect

When a fluid (a liquid or gas) is not moving, the pressure at a given depth in the fluid, called the static pressure, is the same throughout. When the fluid is moving, however, this is not always the case. If the speed of the moving fluid increases, the pressure exerted by the fluid drops. This is called the venturi effect.

The venturi effect is named for Italian physicist Giovanni Venturi (1746–1822), who first studied it. The venturi effect can be observed using two sheets of paper. If the two sheets are held so that they hang parallel and still, the fluid between them—air—is also still, and the pressure on all parts of the sheets is the same. If the velocity of the air layer between the two sheets is increased by blowing on it, the pressure is decreased (compared to the surrounding atmospheric pressure), and the two sheets will move closer together.

This effect was explained by Swiss mathematician and physicist Daniel Bernoulli (1700–1782) in 1738. He used the theory of the conservation of energy, which states that in any system, energy cannot be created or destroyed. A moving fluid has kinetic energy (because it is moving) and potential energy (because it tends to move under the influence of gravity). At any point in the fluid, the static pressure depends on the height of the fluid above that point. This is a measure of the potential energy of the fluid at that point. The kinetic energy of the fluid, which depends on its velocity (speed in a given direction), produces a dynamic pressure. Provided that energy is not added to or removed from the fluid stream, the total energy is conserved. So, when the kinetic energy (and thus the dynamic pressure) increases as a result of the increased velocity, the potential energy and the static pressure must decrease, so the total energy stays the same.

Bernoulli's explanation works well for fluids that cannot be compressed, such as liquids. For gases, however, it must be remembered that changes in pressure affect the density of the gas.

▼ *This pitot tube on the outside of an aircraft uses the venturi effect to measure air speed. The pitot tube measures both the static air pressure and the dynamic air pressure. The difference between the two pressures can be used to calculate the aircraft's speed.*

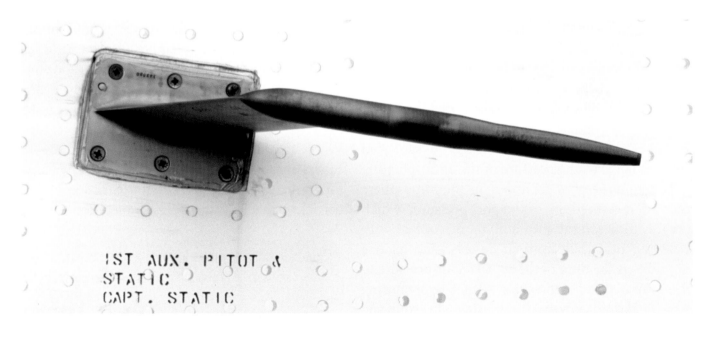

IST AUX. PITOT &
STATIC
CAPT. STATIC

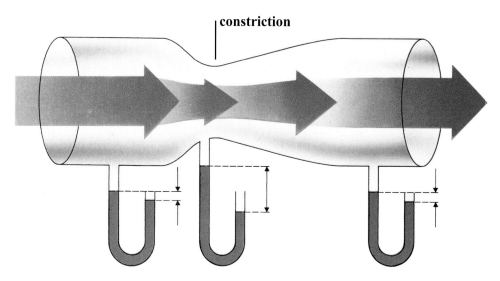

constriction

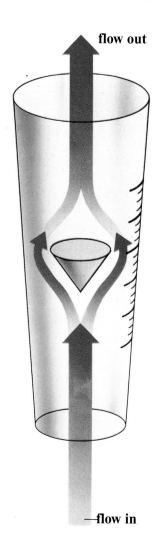

flow out

flow in

Measuring flow rates

Fluid flow rates can be measured using the fact that pressure changes are produced in a fluid in motion. The venturi flowmeter is a device that measures flow rates. It consists of a tube with a smoothly tapered area along its length. When the fluid passes through this area, it speeds up, and the static pressure falls. This drop in static pressure can be measured and thus the flow rate can be determined. The design of the tube shape is very important, since a badly designed tube could cause an unsteady flow of fluid and thus record a false result.

Flow measurements are also made using a rotameter flow gauge. This is a vertical tube that tapers toward the bottom. Inside the tube is a float that sinks to the bottom of the tube when there is no flow past the head of the float. When there is fluid flowing past the head of the float, the float rises, and the flow rate can be calculated.

Air-speed indicators on airplanes rely on the venturi effect. These indicators usually consist of a forward-facing tube, called a pitot tube, connected to a pressure gauge. The tube is surrounded by another tube that is closed at the front but which has a series of holes along its length. The pressure exerted through these holes is a measure of the static air pressure, while the pressure in the pitot tube is a measure of the dynamic pressure. The difference between these two values gives a measure of the forward speed of the airplane. The greater the forward speed, the greater the difference in pressures.

These illustrations show two devices for measuring flow rate: a venturi meter (above) and a rotameter flow gauge (right). The venturi meter works by measuring the pressure drop through the narrow area (constriction) of the tube. The rotameter flow gauge works by noting the height of the float in the tube.

Airfoils and spinning balls

An airfoil (the shape of a cross section of an airplane wing) is more curved on its top surface than on its bottom. When the airfoil moves through the air, the rate of airflow is greater over the top surface. This results in a difference in pressure over the two surfaces, which produce an upward force called lift.

The airflow is also greater on one side of a spinning ball than the other. When a ball traveling horizontally is also made to spin around its vertical axis, it is subjected to a sideways force because of the pressure differences that arise from the different flow rates. This is what happens when a golfer "slices" the ball. It goes off to the right instead of straight ahead.

See also: AERODYNAMICS • PRESSURE • ROCKET

Venus

After the Sun and the Moon, Venus is the brightest object in the sky. It is nearly the same size as Earth but is very much hotter and has a dense, suffocating atmosphere. The surface of Venus is covered with volcanoes and is permanently shrouded in thick clouds.

Venus was named by the ancient Romans after their goddess of love and beauty. The planet is one of the easiest celestial bodies to recognize in the sky. At certain times, Venus can be seen shining brightly in the east just before dawn. Then it is called the morning star. At other times, Venus is visible in the west just after sunset, when it is called the evening star.

Venus is one of the four dense, rocky terrestrial planets that lies between Earth and the Sun. It is an inferior planet, which means the orbit of Venus around the Sun is smaller than Earth's orbit. Venus travels in an almost perfect circle, taking a little under 225 days to do so. The average distance of Venus from the Sun is about 67 million miles (108 million kilometers). At times, the orbit of Venus carries the planet to within 25 million miles (40 million kilometers) of Earth. This is closer than any other celestial body except the Moon and the occasional wayward asteroid.

Phases of Venus

When Venus is observed from Earth during its 225-day "year," its appearance changes all the time. Sometimes it is seen as a slim crescent. At other times, the whole disk is visible. These gradual changes in the appearance of Venus are called its phases. As Venus moves around the Sun, more or less of its surface facing Earth is illuminated.

Venus is in full view when it is farthest from Earth and lies almost directly in line with Earth and the Sun, on the opposite side of the Sun. In this position, Venus is said to be in superior conjunction. It is "new" when it is closest and lies directly between Earth and the Sun, a position known as inferior conjunction.

Occasionally (about twice every 125 years), Venus crosses the face of the Sun when viewed from Earth, a movement that is called a transit.

The cloudy atmosphere

Viewed through a telescope, Venus is a brilliant, yellow-white, featureless globe. Its surface is covered by thick clouds, and it is these highly reflective clouds that make Venus appear so bright. In the past, the clouds prevented scientists from studying the surface of Venus. As a result, scientists could not determine how long the planet took to rotate, and thus the length of its day.

▲ *This computer graphic of Venus was compiled using radar images sent back by the Magellan and Venera space probes.*

▲ **Mariner 2** *was the first successful interplanetary spacecraft. Launched in August 1962, it passed within 21,000 miles (34,000 kilometers) of Venus and first recorded the planet's hot atmosphere.*

Since the 1960s, however, Venus's clouds have been penetrated by radar. Radio waves sent out from radio telescopes can pierce the cloud screen and bounce off the planet's surface. These radio waves are used to create maps of the surface. Using the giant telescope at Arecibo in Puerto Rico, scientists discovered that Venus's rotation period is 243 Earth days. This means that a "day" on Venus is longer than its "year." They also discovered that Venus rotates on its axis in a retrograde (opposite) direction from the other planets. In other words, it spins from east to west.

More advanced radar mapping from Earth and from space probe missions such as the Soviet Venera and U.S. Pioneer missions in the 1970s and 1980s revealed further information about the planet. Later, in 1989, the space probe *Magellan*—the first planetary aircraft to be launched from a space shuttle—began to orbit Venus. Radar images sent back by *Magellan* showed active volcanoes on the planet and provided evidence that the surface of Venus is probably around 400 million years old.

These missions have revealed Venus to be a world totally unlike its "twin" planet, Earth. The atmosphere consists mainly of the dense gas carbon dioxide (CO_2). At the surface, the pressure builds up to nearly one hundred times that on Earth. The clouds that shroud the planet seem to be made up

The atmospheric pressure on the surface of Venus is so dense that it is similar to the pressure of water 3,000 feet (900 meters) below the surface of Earth's oceans. The upper cloud layers move much faster than hurricane-force winds on Earth, sweeping around the planet in just four days. The surface is very still, however, with only very gentle winds.

▼ *This computer simulation shows Maat Mons, which is one of the largest volcanoes on Venus. Lava flows for hundreds of miles across the plains in the foreground.*

of droplets—but not of water as on Earth. The droplets consist of sulfuric acid (H_2SO_4) and have distinctive dark markings, with complex swirling patterns near the equator and dark, V-shaped bands that open up to the west.

The thick, dense atmosphere has a strong effect on the temperature and creates a hostile world. It allows energy to come through from the Sun, which heats up the surface. However, the heat from the surface cannot get out through the atmosphere—instead it acts like a greenhouse. The "greenhouse effect" pushes up the surface temperature to 932°F (500°C) or more. At such temperatures, even lead would melt. In fact, Venus is hotter than Mercury, the planet closest to the Sun. There is unlikely to be seasonal variation in this heat because of the slow,

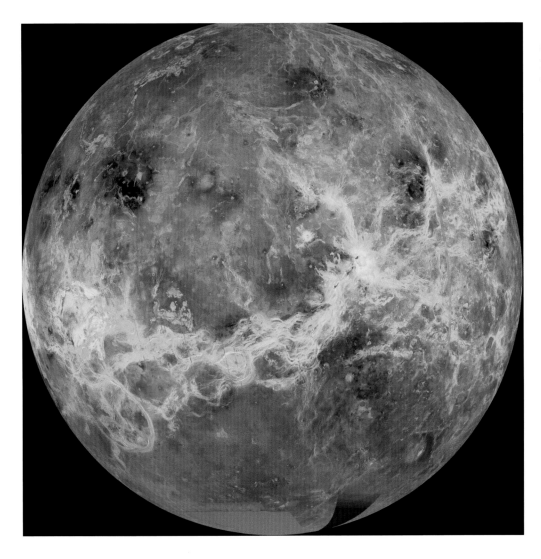

◀ *False-color imagery reveals the different features on the surface of Venus.*

retrograde motion of the planet. Furthermore, because the clouds only allow about 15 percent of the Sun's light to reach the planet's surface, the days on Venus are dim and overcast.

The surface of Venus

Radar mapping has revealed that Venus has no oceans—its surface is covered by a dry, rocky landscape formed by millions of years of volcanic activity. There are rolling plains, lowland areas, and two continent-sized highlands known as Ishtar Terra and Aphrodite Terra. On Ishtar, a large mountain chain rises more than 6 miles (9.6 kilometers) high. There are also rift valleys and impact craters. The Mead Crater is one of the best-preserved large impact craters in the universe. Venus is also dotted with many volcanoes, one thousand of which measure more than 12 miles (20 kilometers) across, although

most are inactive. Maat Mons is one of the largest volcanoes on Venus—it is around 124 miles (200 kilometers) across and 6 miles (9 kilometers) high.

Scientists have measured the density of Venus, and it is similar to Earth's density. Although there is no direct evidence, based on the similar densities, scientists think Venus may have a similar interior to Earth. They think it has a metallic core that extends outward about 1,865 miles (3,000 kilometers) from the planet's center. Similar to Earth's core, the core of Venus probably consists of iron and nickel and a lighter substance, such as sulfur. The mantle, which makes up the bulk of the planet, is dense and molten. Again, like Earth, Venus has a thin crust, but it is unlikely to have tectonic plates.

See also: MOON • SOLAR SYSTEM • SPACE PROBE

Videophone

Videophones enable live, two-way video communication between telephone users via digital cameras built into their telephone handsets. Video calling makes communication both practical and fun. Video callers can see people and show objects, surroundings, and activities in real time as they talk.

In the last century, videophones were objects of science fiction. Now, there are two main technologies that enable video telephone calls—communications satellites and third generation, or 3G, mobile technology.

Communications satellites and videophones

Satellite videophone technology is used by broadcast organizations to beam live action around the world. A satellite is any object that revolves around a planet in an orbit. Although anything orbiting Earth is technically a satellite, the term is typically used to describe a useful object placed in orbit to perform a specific task. Weather satellites, communication satellites, and scientific satellites are the most common.

Communications satellites allow telephone and video conversations to be relayed across the world. The most important feature of a communications satellite is a radio that receives a conversation at one frequency and then amplifies it and retransmits it back to Earth on another frequency. Images from a camera on the videophone are digitally compressed, and the data is beamed by a transmitter to the communications satellite in space. The satellite then sends the signal onto a receiving device located elsewhere.

Television crews are equipped with briefcase-sized videophones and satellite dishes that connect to video cameras. War correspondents can move quickly and discretely with military units and continue broadcasting in the harshest of conditions. Live television pictures give worldwide audiences a view of events as they unfold.

▶ *The telephone is no longer used only for talking. It can now be combined with a real-time video so people making or receiving telephone calls can see images of each other.*

▶ *Videophone technology is advancing quickly, as shown by this hand-held videophone. The increased use of miniaturization will soon lead to videophones being built into wristwatches.*

Satellite videophones that are suitable for general consumers are also available. One type of consumer satellite videophone is a compact desktop device that allows person-to-person video calls over a broadband Internet connection. This removes the need for the user to have a bulky satellite dish for transmitting calls.

In addition to its live video functionality and the ability to operate as a normal voice call unit, the satellite videophone incorporates video conferencing. Businesses, emergency services, and consumers are using this technology to enhance their communications. Routine business travel is often unnecessary when meetings can be conducted by videophone rather than in person. For emergency services, having the ability to transmit live images from the scene of an incident to headquarters is beneficial. Domestic users may rarely visit family members living around the world; the videophone allows them to see their family while speaking on the phone.

3G videophones

Video capability is a key feature of 3G cell phones. 3G is a telecommunications specification for the third generation of mobile communications technology. 3G standards and technologies are used to increase data speed and enhance performance on 3G cell-phone networks. In addition to video calling, the user can view video clips from an enhanced e-mail service and from instant messaging.

As cell phone use has expanded, the existing networks have begun to creak under the strain. A new radio spectrum with increased bandwidth capacity gives telecommunications operators room to expand their services. Existing cellular systems run either on the crowded 800 MHz (megahertz) and 900 MHz wavebands or at the less crowded 1,800 MHz and 1,900 MHz wavebands. 3G systems operate at 2 GHz (gigahertz), a waveband that is cleared of existing traffic. They also make more efficient use of the available spectrum because all base stations can use the same frequency.

With 3G, each video conversation is chopped up into separate "packets". Every packet is labeled with a code that identifies the conversation and eliminates interference. The packets are then transmitted together enabling the network to reassemble them into continuous speech.

Using packets of information to carry data means that the phone is always connected to the network. Messages and e-mails are delivered anytime with no need to dial up. This radical change means 3G mobile networks can support lots more subscribers and let them download data much faster. The upper limit for 3G networks is 2 megabits per second (Mbps) if the user is standing still and 384 kilobits per second (Kbps) on the move. By comparison, second-generation networks transfer data at a much slower 9.6 Kbps.

Video calling using mobile technology requires a larger screen than that of a normal cell phone. The handsets are also slightly bigger to hold the batteries and keys needed to support the new uses.

See also: SATELLITE • TELECOMMUNICATIONS

Virtual reality

Virtual reality (VR) is the illusion of being in a completely different world, for example, on another planet, in the crater of an active volcano, or even inside the body of another human being. Computer-generated sights and sounds trick the brain into thinking the experience is real.

When people go to a movie theater to see the latest film, it is easy to become absorbed in the plot and forget about the real world. However realistic a film might look, though, a viewer remains detached from the action. The filmgoer cannot engage with the onscreen world, and the edges of the screen are always clearly visible. Virtual reality (VR) is an interactive artificial environment in which the user experiences computer-generated sights, sounds, and tactile (touch) information. The user may be able to move around objects and even pick them up—the user's actions determine what happens in the virtual world.

A typical VR system has a helmet and a glove for one or both hands. Two small television screens are mounted in the helmet, one in front of each eye. These present pictures of the imaginary world. (In computer science, the word *virtual* means "created or simulated by a computer.") Because each screen shows the slightly different view that the corresponding eye would see if the virtual world were real, the user experiences a three-dimensional, or stereoscopic, scene. Sensors in the helmet detect movements of the head and instantly change the scenes shown on the television screens. Headphones in the helmet may also provide sounds for the virtual world.

In some VR systems, sensors also detect movements of the feet and legs, so the screens in the helmet can show the virtual world as if the user is walking through it. The glove or gloves detect the movement of the fingers, so the user can pick up

▼ *Children play in a virtual world at the Joyopolis Virtual Reality Arcade in Tokyo, Japan. VR transports people into an environment of computer-generated sights and sounds, stimulating the senses into believing the experience is real.*

imaginary objects, seeing a "virtual hand" reaching out and grasping the objects. The VR glove has another important function. Built-in motors offer resistance to the fingers. As the user clasps an imaginary cup, for example, the glove lets his or her fingers close until they seem to be in contact with the cup. On the screens, the user will see the fingers close around the cup. At the same time, the user will not be able to bring the fingers together any closer. If the user tries to pick up an egg, he or she will have to do it gently. The VR glove allows the fingers to close around the egg, and the screens will show the egg smashing. Advanced VR systems of the future might even provide the gooey feeling of the egg covering the hands as it breaks.

Degrees of immersiveness

The more sensory stimulation that a VR system provides, the more immersive the system is said to be. The more advanced the system is, the greater the degree of immersiveness. A video game, for example, provides partial immersion. The user moves around a virtual world, affecting the world by pressing buttons. The scene changes to show the user what he or she would see when running, turning around, shooting, and so on. Being able to walk through the virtual world is a further degree of immersion. Some of the flight-simulation or

DID YOU KNOW?

Many people do not like the implications of virtual reality. They argue that it provides people with a way of performing actions they would not otherwise consider in real life. In the movie *Minority Report* (2002), which is based on a novel by Philip K. Dick and stars Tom Cruise, a company illegally offers customers the chance to live out their fantasies of criminal acts, such as murdering a hated boss.

driving-simulation games in an arcade add another dimension: the seat tilts, turns, and vibrates according to what the user is doing onscreen.

VR and real world combined

VR helmets have been developed for use in warplanes. The pilot sees the world outside the cockpit in the normal way, but instrument readings, radar images, and images of targets on the ground are projected onto the visor of the pilot's helmet, so he or she does not have to turn away from the scene outside to look at the flight instruments. The virtual reality here consists of computer-generated images combined with an ordinary view of the land and sky outside.

Robotic craft can be piloted with VR systems when it is not possible for people to make the trip. For example, robot submarines, similar to those

| **DID YOU KNOW?** |
VR helped to test a drug intended to combat vertigo (a sense of dizziness). People who had taken the drug were given the simulated experience of traveling in a glass elevator. The dizziness they felt was measured and compared with the dizziness felt by people making the same elevator ride but without taking the drug. The new drug was found to be effective.

used to explore the wreck of the sunken liner *Titanic,* are often guided by people wearing VR helmets and using controls similar to those used to play video games. In this case, the scene displayed to the user is a view of the real world, not a computer-generated virtual environment.

Medical applications

VR systems have many applications in medicine. People who have phobias (intense fears that interfere with their lives) can be taught to lose these fears using VR. For example, someone may have a phobia of flying in an airliner. Using VR, they can be taken through a realistic experience of going on a flight. They will probably feel less anxiety because they know the experience is not real, but if they do have a panic attack, it is easy to stop the session.

Patients with bad burns have been provided with VR helmets to provide distraction during painful medical treatment. The distractions have even included snow scenes to suggest coolness and to take their minds away from the original fire experience.

Surgeons use VR systems to create images of the insides of their patients before and during surgery. The surgical team can see hugely magnified images of the organs on which they are working. They manipulate hand controls that, in turn, control the

◄ *Military and civilian pilots are trained in flight simulators, which are VR systems. The trainee pilot sits in a dummy cockpit, and the computer-generated images of the world outside the cockpit respond to the movements of the controls.*

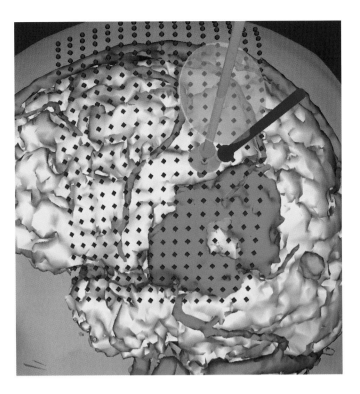

▶ *Virtual reality is used to map the brain before surgery to remove a tumor (green). Blood vessels are shown in red. The images are created using coils (red and blue rods, top right), which fire pulses of electricity into the brain at given points. The map is created by measuring the brain's response to the pulses. This process allows the surgeon to correctly attack the tumor without damaging healthy brain tissue.*

surgical instruments. The delicate movements of the surgeon's hands may be translated into even more precise movements of robotic instruments, making possible procedures that would be difficult for the unaided surgeon.

Pharmaceutical applications

Medical scientists use VR systems to design new drugs. The user wears a VR helmet and gloves to look at magnified images of particular molecules. At first, this is probably the molecule of some existing drug. Such a molecule is usually complex, consisting of hundreds or thousands of atoms. Most new drugs are designed by making small changes to the molecular structure of existing drugs. The scientist will try to make changes to the molecule, perhaps by adding a smaller group of atoms. Different atoms will combine with others more or less readily, and the VR user will feel forces resisting or helping his or her attempts to place the new group of atoms on the existing molecule.

DID YOU KNOW?

Egyptian mummies are the embalmed and bandaged remains of Egyptian kings and queens who died thousands of years ago. Unwrapping the mummies would damage the fragile remains beyond repair. It is now possible to create images of the insides of mummies without damaging them. X-rays are passed through the mummy from all directions, and the X-ray images are processed using a computer. The resulting three-dimensional image can be made into a VR environment.

Sometimes the scientist will not be able to add the smaller group of atoms. Other times, the user will find a spot to place the smaller group of atoms where it seems likely to produce the desired effect. Then it is necessary to make the new molecule in reality and test it on real people.

The future of VR

VR was heavily publicized in the 1980s but then became less popular. Advances in technology should improve VR in the future. Gloves and helmets are getting lighter and therefore less tiring to use. These devices and the computers controlling them are getting faster, eliminating the delay between an action and the response in the virtual environment. This avoids the motion sickness that sometimes afflicted users in the past.

Other ways of improving the design of VR systems are also being discovered. For example, not being able to glance down to see the body can make it hard for a user to judge his or her orientation in space. Simply providing a virtual body can make this aspect of VR much more satisfying to use.

See also: COMPUTER • ROBOTICS • SURGERY

Virus, biological

Viruses are tiny germs that cause diseases. They enter living cells and make the cells grow new viruses. The cell are then killed or damaged. Viruses are so simple that without living cells they would not be able to live themselves. They cause many diseases that are difficult to cure.

The discovery of bacteria led to a better understanding of the causes of illness and new methods of prevention. It was found that bacteria could be removed from a liquid by passing it through a fine filter (a very fine sieve). The holes in the filter were so small that they stopped the tiny bacteria from passing through it.

However, some disease-causing organisms were still able to pass through the bacterial filters. These organisms were obviously even smaller than bacteria. Scientists now know that these tiny organisms are viruses, although it was not until the invention of powerful electron microscopes that it was possible to see a virus.

What are viruses?

Viruses are perhaps the simplest form of life, although some people say that they are not living at all. They do contain nucleic acids, either deoxyribonucleic acid (DNA) or ribonucleic acid (RNA), although no virus carries both. Nucleic acids contain the chemical codes for all living characteristics. They carry genetic information from generation to generation in all living things. DNA is passed on when cells divide, as well as during reproduction, and this DNA ends up in the nucleus of each living cell. DNA passes

▼ *This image shows human skin infected with the smallpox variola virus. The name smallpox is derived from the Latin word for "spotted" and refers to the bumps that appear on the body of an infected person.*

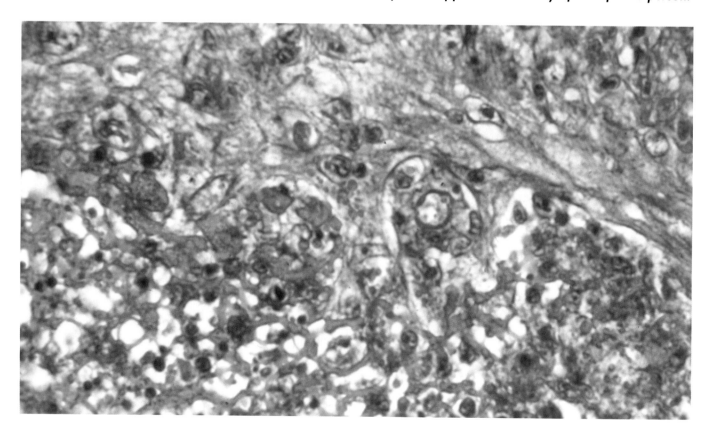

▼ *These illustrations show different types of viruses. Viruses come in many different shapes and sizes and vary considerably in their level of complexity. Almost all viruses that infect human cells are roughly spherical in shape. Viruses infect all forms of life, including mammals, insects, fish, and plants. Some viruses even attack bacteria.*

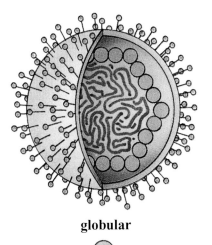

globular

helical

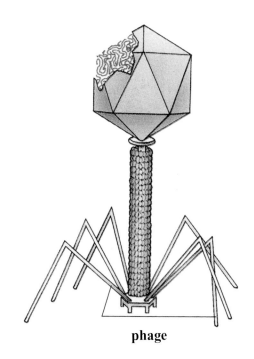

phage

icosahedron

"messages" to the chemical "factories" in the cells, telling them to make various chemicals at various times. These messages are carried by RNA.

Although viruses contain DNA or RNA, they do not consist of much else other than protein. The protein forms a capsule or jacket that contains the thread of nucleic acid.

Structure of viruses

The size of viruses is measured in nanometers (there are 25,400,000 nanometers in one inch). The smallest viruses are 20 or 30 nanometers across, and even the smallpox viruses (the largest viruses) are only 200 to 300 nanometers across.

At the center of each virus is a strand of nucleic acid, either DNA or RNA but never both. This is coiled inside a protein capsule consisting of individual "building blocks." These blocks are called capsomeres, and it is the way in which the capsomeres fall into place around the strand that gives the virus particle its basic shape.

Many viruses are almost completely round, although detailed examination shows that they have 20 equal flat sides. This structure is known as an icosahedron. Many plant viruses are shaped like a hollow tube, the rabies virus is bullet shaped, the smallpox virus is brick shaped, and some viruses that infect bacteria resemble tadpoles, with big heads and long tails.

Some viruses, such as the influenza viruses, have a bristlelike envelope around the protein capsule. This gives them a lumpy appearance under the electron microscope.

How do viruses multiply?

Viruses cannot multiply unless they invade a living cell. First, they are absorbed by the surface of the cell and taken inside the cell. The genetic material of the virus—the nucleic acid—is then released into the cell and mixes with the cell's own genetic material. This allows the viral genetic material to take over the cell.

The viral nucleic acid stops the cell from making its own proteins and nucleic acids. Instead, the cell starts to produce viral proteins and viral genetic material. These are then assembled inside the cell until the cell contains many new viruses, all made using the cell's chemical "factories." The last stage of the process is when the cell, now dead, starts to fall apart and releases all the new viruses to infect more living cells.

If a virus does not find a living cell, it cannot multiply. If it is in a place that is too hot or too dry, for example, it will be killed and will not be able to infect any more cells. Some viruses, however, are very tough and can still be infectious (able to cause disease) even if they have been lying around in dry, dusty conditions for a long time.

Spread of viruses

Viruses are extremely infectious and are easily transmitted. Until measles vaccination was introduced, it was almost certain that every child in the country would get measles once a major epidemic started. When smallpox was common, it was possible to catch the disease merely by coming into contact with a sick person's infected clothing.

Viruses can be spread in different ways. Many viruses are transmitted by droplet infection—the common cold, influenza, and measles viruses are all spread in this way. The viruses infect the throat and nose and cause the cells there to produce a lot of mucus. This mucus contains millions of viruses produced by the infected cells. Whenever the sick person coughs or sneezes, a fine spray of mucus droplets is shot into the air, each droplet containing the infectious viruses. Anyone standing in range is bound to breathe in the droplets, thus catching the disease. It is therefore always better to cough or sneeze into a handkerchief to trap as many virus particles as possible.

Polio and hepatitis viruses and the enteroviruses (which infect the intestines) enter the body through the wall of the intestines. These viruses are passed out of the body in the feces of the infected person, and they can be picked up by other people if there is poor hygiene or an insanitary water supply. If the water supply is clean and disinfected, the excreted viruses are killed and cannot infect other people.

Other viruses are carried by insects and enter the human body when the insect bites a person. The West Nile virus, for example, is transmitted by mosquitoes. Many animal viruses are also transmitted by insect bites.

An open cut can be a route for a virus to enter a body. The rabies virus, which infects humans and animals such as dogs and foxes, enters the body when an infected animal bites or licks an open cut.

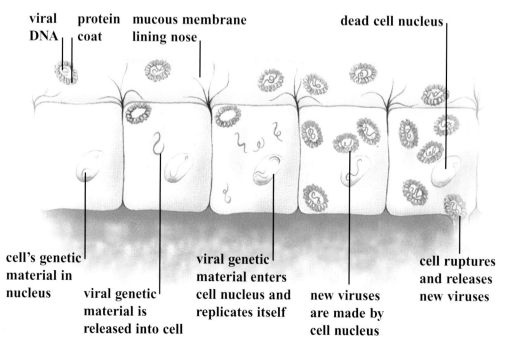

viral DNA | protein coat | mucous membrane lining nose | dead cell nucleus

cell's genetic material in nucleus

viral genetic material is released into cell

viral genetic material enters cell nucleus and replicates itself

new viruses are made by cell nucleus

cell ruptures and releases new viruses

◄ *This diagram shows the process by which a virus takes over a cell. First, the virus is absorbed into the cell. Then the genetic material of the virus mixes with the cell's genetic material, and the virus takes over the cell. The cell is then used to produce new viruses. Eventually, the cell dies and new viruses are released, ready to invade more cells.*

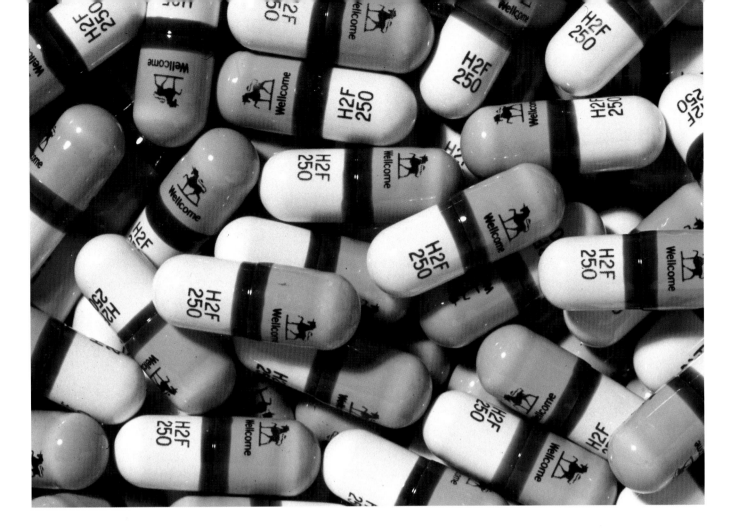

▲ *These drugs were developed to slow down the development of the human immunodeficiency virus (HIV). The HIV virus can lie dormant inside the body for years, but at some point it becomes active, and the full-blown form of the disease, called acquired immune deficiency syndrome (AIDS) develops.*

Growing viruses in the laboratory

Viruses must be grown in laboratories for scientists to study them. Because they do not multiply outside living cells, this has proven difficult. It was then discovered that viruses could be grown inside fertilized chickens' eggs. If material containing the viruses is injected into the eggs, many tiny damaged areas develop, each area of damage coming from one virus.

It is now possible to grow cells in the laboratory from various parts of animals, for instance, hamster kidney cells. These are grown in glass bottles and form a flat surface on the glass. If viruses are allowed to infect these sheets of cells, they produce small damaged areas where the cells are killed. Each area is produced by one virus.

Prevention and cure of viral infections

Some of the best methods of preventing viral infection are simple health measures, such as washing hands and covering cuts. Vaccination is the best defense against a viral epidemic. A vaccination against measles, for example, will build up a person's immune (disease-fighting) system against that disease. If the immune system later comes in contact with that virus, it will be able to fight it off.

Once a person is infected, however, it is impossible to stop the multiplication of the viruses. They are "protected" inside the cells they take over.

The only exceptions are infections with herpes virus, which cause inflammatory diseases of the skin. Such infections can be treated with a new drug called acyclovir. This drug attacks only the cells infected with herpes, leaving normal cells untouched.

See also: BACTERIA • CELL • ELECTRON MICROSCOPE • GENETICS • PARASITOLOGY • VACCINATION

Glossary

Anode The positive electrode in an electrochemical cell; the electrode toward which anions (negatively charged ions) migrate.

Bacteria Single-celled organisms most of which are decomposers, but many of which are responsible for infectious diseases in plants, animals, and people.

Cathode The negative electrode in an electrochemical cell; the electrode toward which cations (positively charged ions) migrate.

Conductor A substance or medium (such as liquid or gas) that conducts heat, light, sound, or especially an electrical charge.

Density Quantity representing the mass of a substance, distribution of a quantity, or the number of individuals per unit of volume, area, or length.

Diffuse For particles in liquids and gases to move from areas of high concentration to areas of lower concentration so that the particles become more evenly distributed.

Electrolysis The process by which the passage of an electrical current through a solution or a molten ionic compound brings about a chemical change.

Electrolyte Solution or pure liquid that contains anions and cations. The passage of an electrical current can cause an electrolyte to decompose.

Electroplating Process of coating with metal by means of an electrical current. Plating metal may be transferred to nonconductive surfaces by first coating them with a conductive base layer.

Frequency The rate at which something happens or is repeated, as in the number of pulses in radio waves or the number of times an alternating current flows back and forth.

Gravity The natural force of attraction exerted by a massive body, such as Earth, upon objects at or near its surface, tending to draw the objects toward the center of the body.

Horsepower A unit of power equal to 745.7 watts or 33,000 foot-pounds per minute. Used, in particular, to rate the power of engines.

Insulator Object or medium (such as a liquid or gas) with an unusually low capacity to conduct electrical current, heat, or sound.

Isotope Any of two or more forms of a chemical element with the same atomic number but different atomic masses.

Kinetic energy Energy possessed by a moving object or a particle. Kinetic energy depends not only on the motion of an object or particle, but also on its mass.

Mantle Thick middle layer of Earth (or other rocky planet) between the crust and the core, composed of dense, rocky matter.

Mass Amount of matter in a body, which is measured as the body's inertia or resistance to being moved and is distinct from its weight.

Microorganism An organism, such as a bacterium, that is too small to be seen by the naked eye.

Oscillate To swing back and forth between alternate extremes with a steady, uninterrupted rhythm, usually within a definable period of time.

Pendulum A body suspended from a fixed point so that it can swing back and forth under the influence of gravity. Pendulums are used to regulate the movement of clocks.

Radar Short for "radio detection and ranging." Equipment used to locate the position and velocity of distant objects using narrow beams of high-frequency radio or microwave pulses.

Radiation Energy radiated or transmitted as rays, waves, or in the form of particles. X-rays and visible light are examples of radiation.

Richter scale Open-ended logarithmic scale used to express the amount of energy released by earthquakes.

Solvent A substance that breaks down or dissolves another substance.

Turbine A wheel driven by moving water, steam, or gas, usually used to work engines and generators.

Weight The force with which a body is attracted to Earth or another celestial body, equal to the product of the object's mass and the acceleration of gravity.

Index

Page numbers in **bold** refer to main articles; those in *italics* refer to illustrations.